Gap Year, American Style

Journeys Toward Learning, Serving, and Self-Discovery

ISBN-10: 0615846793
ISBN-13: 978-0-615-84679-8

Cover and design by Rachel Austen Anderson and Michael Wolff
Cover photo courtesy of *Carpe Diem Education*

CONTENTS

"Go. Do. Be."
-Julia Bloch, Gap Year Alum

Introduction 1

Chapter One: Gap Year Fundamentals 6

Gap Year Q&A 9

Origins of the Gap Year 13

Gap Year, American Style Research 18

Chapter Two: Journeys in Time 23

Why Do I Want to Go to College? 24

Narrowing Gap Year Options 26

Logistics 29

Individual Journeys 30

Growth through Adversity 45

Reverse Culture Shock 48

Transitioning Voices 51

Gap Year Survey Findings Summary 55

Tips 55

Chapter Three: Learning and Education 57

Time Out or Burn Out 65
Will They Return to College? 67
About Deferrals 68
Access to vs. Success in College 71
Gap Years and Educational Direction 79
Gap Year Survey Findings Summary 85
Tips 86

Chapter Four: Gap Year Dollars and Sense 89

Is It Worth It? 90
Paying for Gap Years 97
If a Gap Year Costs Money, Who Pays? 100
Costs and Benefits 111
Gap Year Survey Findings Summary 116
Tips 117

Chapter Five: Gappers in the Workplace 119

Research on Gap Years and Employability from the UK 121
U.S. – UK Gapper Competency Comparison 128
Gap Years and Employability 133
Broadening Skills Employers Value 136
Expanded Networks 140
Job Satisfaction 142
Gap Year Survey Findings Summary 147
Tips 148

Chapter Six: Volunteering and Service 150

AmeriCorps Survey 153
Gap Year Survey. 155
Does Volunteering Continue? 161
Volunteering and Careers. 163
Gap Year Survey Findings Summary 168
Tips 169

Chapter Seven: Global Citizenship 170

Perceptions of Americans Abroad 182
Gap Years and Study Abroad Experiences. 185
Tourists vs. Wanderers 191
Experiencing Anti-Americanism 193
Parents' Insights 197
Gap Year Survey Findings Summary 204
Tips 206

Chapter Eight: Gappers Look in the Mirror 207

Self-Awareness. 211
Growth In Competency Terms 214
Reflecting, Blogs, and Journals 218
Parents Look In the Mirror 223
The Journey as Narrative 226
Gap Year Survey Findings Summary 230
Tips 231

Chapter Nine: Continuing the Journey **232**

Appendix: Gap Year Partners **241**

Programs, Consulting Partners, and Experts 241
Survey and Research Partners 248

Gap Year Bibliography **250**

Acknowledgments **256**

About the Authors **258**

Index **259**

INTRODUCTION

Approximately seventy percent of high school seniors will attend college the fall after they graduate, according to the Bureau of Labor Statistics. That means that almost one million students will not proceed directly to additional formal education.

Some of these young adults will head to the workplace, perhaps pursuing higher education at a future date. Others will delay college plans and invest time working and saving money to help pay for further education. A number will choose to take time off after high school because they feel burned out after years focused on accumulating credentials to compete for college acceptance. Still others will try to discover more about themselves, or the world outside of their "comfort zone," before working or continuing their education.

An option for some of these young men and women is to take a gap year – or a planned break before or during college – to invest time performing community service, studying, traveling, or working in the United States or abroad.

We personally connected with the gap year option when our youngest son, Adam, suggested that he was not ready to go to college after graduating from high school. As a high school principal more than two decades earlier, Karl (Adam's dad) had counseled students who were at risk of dropping out about the potential of gap year experiences. Recalling the positive impact of a "real-world education" that gap years offered to his students in the 1980s, we were interested in Adam's motives and his plans.

Adam told us that a student who had graduated from his high school, Matt Hendren, had returned to share his experiences in a community service program called City Year. City Year brings together young people from a variety of backgrounds to develop skills and earn money for college, while giving back through community service. Matt, like Adam, had attended a public high school in North Carolina and had been accepted to college. Matt chose to defer formal education in favor of service in Boston, where he taught elementary students and lived on a modest living stipend provided by the program. The experience had been transformational. Matt wanted other students to know there were alternatives to what many consider a traditional path from high school to and through college.

We watched and supported Adam as he developed his own gap year plan. After learning there was limited space and time to apply to City Year, the idea was that Adam (who had never traveled out of the country or west of the Mississippi River) would work to help pay for travel to Costa Rica. There he would live with a local family and teach English to young students in a mountain village. He then would go to New Zealand where he and a team of his peers would help tend an environmental preserve. Adam's direction changed as his view of the world and he grew during these first months of living his gap year plan. He then chose to study animals and plant life in the Smoky Mountains of North Carolina and teach outdoor education in Texas, for which he was paid and provided with room and board. Also integrated into his plan was additional time to work and save money, and re-applying to college.

The set of gap experiences before attending college impacted Adam in ways that he is still discovering. The self-awareness and world view echoed the type of growth we hear about from other gap students and parents. Adam developed a sense of confidence and maturity and expanded a foundation of sensitivity and perspective. He grew into a proactive learner. He discovered an academic and career direction as an environmental scientist that probably would have remained nascent if he'd proceeded directly into a college classroom.

We have had the opportunity to talk widely – both formally and through informal conversations – on the gap year option. We've run into the advocates (a number of students, parents, educators, reporters, and opinion leaders who believe the gap year is a positive option that should be considered more widely in the United States). We've listened to the skeptics (those who believe the gap option offers little or no benefit and may threaten to de-rail young Americans from the traditional path to adulthood). And we've talked with those who haven't heard of, or aren't familiar, with gap years.

The topic, however, almost always sparks interesting and lively conversation. And almost every conversation cycles back to the question, variously phrased: "What is the impact of a gap year?"

Based on our experience with Adam and interviews with dozens of gap year alums and parents, we wrote a book, *The Gap-Year Advantage: Helping Your Child Benefit from Time Off Before or During College* (St. Martin's Griffin, 2005). The book includes advice, tips, and information for parents and students as they develop and implement a gap-year strategy.

As educators who have been involved in public policy at the federal, state, and local levels – and as gap year parents – we began exploring information that was available on the broader impact of gap years. Finding limited quantitative or structured qualitative information on the topic, we decided to conduct a first step to collect information on how time off with a purpose before or during college influences young adults.

Whereas *The Gap-Year Advantage* is designed to address the *how* of developing a gap year plan, *Gap Year, American Style* is dedicated to the *why* in terms of the impact of gap years. Building on an established interest in experiential learning as a supplement to traditional classroom education, we have had the opportunity to connect with hundreds of gap year students, parents, counselors, and program directors in conducting initial research.

The majority echo what we observed in Adam – that structured time away before college can help some teenagers emerge into more mature, resilient, and compassionate young adults. They also observe that the experiences can translate into a more meaningful time in college that tends to resonate for years beyond. That is not to say that young adults stepping out into the world for the first time don't face challenges. They do. Or that every gap experience goes as imagined or planned. They don't. Or that parents aren't nervous about their child's stepping out into the world or whether they will return to college. They are. But gap alums will tell you that the process of overcoming challenges is an important part of the experience that spurs growth and resilience, in many cases resulting in greater maturity than college-bound peers.

The research we have conducted includes an online survey of more than 300 students to explore the impact of gap years in areas such as education, financial awareness, work and employment, community service, global citizenship, and self-discovery. It also includes in-depth interviews with dozens of students and their parents.

The observations from this investigation, and particularly from the reflections of gap year alums, are offered in this book. They are offered with an upfront caveat that this is not a comprehensive research study by any means. There is not a baseline or control group and the gap year alums who responded to our survey self-selected to participate. The purpose of the observations is to provide a snapshot of the potential impact of gap years that might stimulate more formal and comprehensive research. We also hope to add a chapter to the broader conversation about the journey young Americans take on the road to maturity and adulthood. Along the way, we hope that the stories of gappers, tips and ideas for taking a gap year experience and making the most of the journey will be of interest to students (and their parents) considering taking a road less traveled.

Chapter One

GAP YEAR FUNDAMENTALS

OFF TRACK OR FINDING A PATH?

"I mark myself in terms of my gap year; the before, during, and after are rather different people. My gap year works as a foundation for my life away from home, away from high school. It helped prepare me for college life as well as the 'real world.' All the experiences, mistakes, and adventures have impacted me in ways I do not even know about yet."

– Megan Kelly

Along our journey as gap-year parents and educators, we have connected with hundreds of gapper alums, each with a unique story to tell. Their collective journey represents an option for students who may be interested in an alternative path to going straight to college after graduating from high school. Their gap experiences illustrate how this option has the potential to help students learn more about themselves and the world, get more out of college and life beyond, and contribute in a more meaningful way to others.

In the pages ahead, you will learn about many of these students and read their reflections on what gap experiences mean to them. To illustrate the journey, here are the stories of Megan Kelly, Teresa Obrero, and Colin Fox.

Megan Kelly

Megan Kelly's gap year journey began when she applied to ten colleges and received nine "thin" envelopes. She wasn't that interested in the one college that accepted her. Her college advisor suggested a gap year – a structured break between high school and college – and "it was the perfect solution." Megan spent the first part of her year at Oxford Tutorial College in the United Kingdom where she studied philosophy and writing in the small classes and one-on-one opportunities with tutors that mark the program. She then traveled to New Zealand where she built houses and took a wilderness seminar. Megan believes gap year experiences "are the best way for a student to find out about themselves while being involved in something that is important to them." Megan attended Emerson College in Boston, Massachusetts.

Teresa Obrero

Teresa Obrero always wanted to go to college, but couldn't afford to. A group of young volunteers from an organization called City Year had done work at her high school in Cleveland, Ohio, and she was intrigued. City Year is a non-profit organization and part of the AmeriCorps organization, dedicated to service and giving back to the community. It also offers a living stipend and an education award to help pay for college, a formula that fit Teresa perfectly. After being accepted to City Year, she began two years of service after high school tutoring elementary school students in Cleveland. Participating in City Year gave Teresa more confidence and the recognition that she is a leader. Teresa attended college while serving through City Year, and became the first in her family to graduate with a higher education degree. "One of the best moments in my life was when I did graduate from college, and having my younger brothers and sisters there to see that college is an option." When we last connected, Teresa was earning a master's degree at the University of Minnesota in non-profit management and social work. She plans to dedicate herself to public policy to help lower-income students have access to college.

Colin Fox

Colin Fox went through his freshman orientation at Clemson University and saw disaster coming if he continued down this well-worn path. He and his mother decided it would be worth exploring alternatives before going any further. They sat down with Neil Bull, founder of the Center for Interim Programs, LLC, and soon discovered that Colin had opportunities for a gap year training sled dogs in Alaska (where he had his "first feeling of accomplishment"). He then attended a rigorous academic and cultural studies program in Greece called ITHAKA. At the completion of a successful year's experience and with strong academic recommendations in hand, Colin was accepted to St. John's College in Annapolis, Maryland. His time there was marked with a change of campuses after his sophomore year – from Annapolis to Santa Fe - from which he graduated. He credits his gap year journey that led him to St. John's for his love of learning that continues today in his job as an executive editor at a major publishing house in New York.

Gap Year Q&A

"Students walk a pre-determined path for eighteen years. Then, just three months out of high school, we expect them to make informed decisions in college that will impact the rest of their lives. That doesn't make any sense, much less common sense."

- Gap Year Parent

As we have spoken with hundreds of parents and students individually and in public and online forums, almost any conversation begins with basic questions. The first one generally is, "What is a gap year?"

What is a gap year?

A working definition of a gap year or gap experience is when a student takes time out before or during college to pursue a structured series of experiences before entering or returning to college. As the examples of Megan Kelly, Teresa Obrero, and Colin Fox illustrate, there are a wide variety – in fact, there are thousands – of options for gappers to undertake. A gap experience can take place over several months, a year, or in some cases longer, and generally involves one or more of the following:

- volunteering or serving in the United States or abroad;
- working or interning in the United States or abroad;
- traveling in the United States or abroad; and/or
- studying in the United States or abroad.

It's a journey, usually taken between high school and college, that involves some sort of a plan, vision, and purpose. These gap experiences do not include students' taking an extended break from formal education to hang out, lounge on the couch, party with friends, or play video games. Nor are they a random set of experiences that occur as one sits by passively and lets life happen.

Gap year experiences involve taking a break from formal education to explore the world and to see yourself from a different perspective – with the intent to enter or return to higher education.

The gappers we connected with had experiences almost as varied as the individuals themselves. You will learn about the breadth and depth of options in the chapters ahead. As one gap alum explained, "If you can dream it, you can do it!"

Why do students take gap years?

The reasons students take a gap year also vary from individual to individual. However, the gap alums we know report there are two top reasons for taking time off:

- students feel a need to take a break from formal education; and
- they want to learn more about themselves.

Given the pressure of the college application process facing many students, it's not surprising that the primary reason for a gap year is that students feel the need for time off. For years, many students (and, in a number of cases, their parents) have worked to improve class rank, increase SAT or ACT scores, and pile on extra-curricular activities – whatever it takes to get into the "right school." In the words of many of the gappers we interviewed, they just get "burned out."

If you think about it, it also makes sense that students want a break to learn more about themselves. For eighteen years (more or less), their existence has largely been defined by instructions and expectations from parents, teachers, coaches, and friends. Now – just three months after finishing high school – they're expected to set out on four (or more) years in college classrooms and begin to make decisions about their personal and academic lives based on relatively limited real-world experience. More than one parent we talked with reflected on how little self-knowledge they had straight out of high school in the 1970s, wishing they had taken a gap experience before passively choosing a major and potential career path. As one parent summarized, "Students walk a pre-determined path for eighteen years. Then, just three months out of high school, we expect them to make informed decisions in college that will impact the rest of their lives. That doesn't make any sense, much less common sense."

Other reasons students seek a gap journey include to:

- help pay for college;
- develop skills;
- explore a potential career path; or
- travel and learn more about the world.

Some believe they lack the focus, direction, or motivation to make the most of college – in some cases, after attending college for a while. We also have heard from students who opt for a gap year because they were not accepted at a college they're interested in attending, had been wait-listed or, in a few cases, had not been accepted at any college. Others may have never viewed college as an option, having no role models, low finances, and receiving little encouragement from family, friends, or counselors to apply.

How much does a gap year cost?

The cost can vary from programs that pay you to those that cost the equivalent of time in college. Cost doesn't correspond to quality so the key is to do research. We explore the cost of gap years and ways to pay for them in an upcoming chapter.

Is the gap year a growing trend in the United States?

The "growing trend" question is usually the first one that reporters ask. The truth is there is no reliable number (as of when we are writing this book) of how many students in the United States take a gap year as we have defined it. But there is strong evidence that the trend is growing. Programs and consultants are seeing an increase in the number of inquiries they receive. Colleges report an increased number of deferrals for gap years. A growing number of colleges are supporting the option. And gap year fairs are appearing around the country. News reports and articles routinely refer to it as a growing trend in America and most counselors, program providers, and many educators agree.

What is the impact of a gap year on students?

The impact of gap years is a topic we try to explore in this book. Anecdotally, gap students report multiple benefits of their time off including gaining:

- self awareness;
- confidence;
- a strong sense of personal responsibility;
- heightened resilience; and
- a level of maturity about learning, work, the world – and themselves.

There also is evidence that gap year students tend to develop a passion for learning, get more out of their education, and do better in school than their peers. However, there is little quantitative information in the United States in this area which is why we conducted some initial gap year research that you'll learn about in this book.

Origins of the Gap Year

Before continuing with the journey, it might be helpful to offer context about the origins of the gap year concept.

It Started with the Brits

It's difficult to place the origin of the term "gap year" exactly, but it appears to be tied to 1977 in the United Kingdom when an organization called the Gap Activity Projects was established. The purpose of the organization was to facilitate programs for students between the British equivalent of high school and college. (The organization has since changed its name to Lattitude Global Volunteering and it specializes in arranging gap programs for young adults from seventeen to twenty-five years of age.)

A gap year industry started to emerge in the UK as programs, travel industry organizations, and insurance companies recognized the opportunity to nurture a promising market. In 1998, entrepreneurs Tom Griffiths and Peter Pedrick (both gap alums) launched a website at GapYear.com, accompanied by a gap year magazine that was distributed to schools and related guides, products, and partnerships that found a lucrative and growing gap clientele.

Then Prince William and Prince Harry took respective gap years in 2000-2001 and 2003-2004. Prince William's gap year included preparing for training with the Welsh Guards in Belize, working as a volunteer in Chile to help construct walkways from logs, teaching in local Chilean schools, working on a dairy farm in the UK, and traveling in Africa. Prince Harry worked on a ranch in Australia, helped at an orphanage for children with AIDS in a small mountain kingdom in Africa, trained with the Rugby Football Union, and spent time learning about land management on a farm in the UK.

Thousands of young Brits followed suit with their own gap years and the concept took off. Today, it is estimated that more than 10 percent of young people in the UK choose a gap year option.

Although British students make up almost half of the international gap year market, the option also is catching on in other countries. Australians (who have started to call it a "personal development year"), New Zealanders, and other Europeans comprise most of the rest. Primary reasons for the increasing trend in these countries include students' wanting workplace experience before higher education, needing time out for exploration, and wanting to be more confident about their academic and career direction before committing to additional studies.

U.S. Gap Traditions

The U.S. gap tradition can be traced to the late Neil Bull and the 1960s. As headmaster of the Verde Valley School in Sedona, Arizona, Neil perceived a positive impact on his students as they served on Navajo reservations and in towns in Mexico as part of their formal education. In 1980, *The New York Times* published an article on gap years that noted Neil's work. Neil subsequently received inquiries from parents who were intrigued by what they read and had questions about a gap option for their sons or daughters. He planted the seeds for interim or gap experiences that began to interest a small number of parents as well as educators: there was an option for students on the road to and through college in taking structured time off.

As he began to advise students and parents on gap year options, he emphasized a student's direct involvement in developing an individualized plan. He believed students should be "dreaming their own dreams and realizing the possibilities," as Mimi Bull, Neil's wife, recalls. In 1980, Neil founded the Center for Interim Studies, LLC, in Cambridge, Massachusetts. The Center is recognized as the first and longest-running independent gap year organization in the United States. Neil's daughter, Holly Bull, is President of Interim today.

Another recognition of a time-off option for U.S. students started more than 30 years ago when Harvard began suggesting gap years as an option in its admissions letters. In an essay that is frequently cited by those making a case for a gap year, "Time Out or Burn Out for the Next Generation" (originally published in 2000 and revised in 2006), Harvard's admissions officers support their recommendation. The authors – William Fitzsimmons, dean of admissions and financial aid; Marlyn McGrath Lewis, director of admissions; and Charles Ducey, director of the bureau of study counsel – based the essay on their observations of applicants over a number of years. The essay points to the pressure to succeed against a baseline of external expectations that affects today's students. Among other developments, the essay suggests, the pressure to succeed has given rise to a track that starts before pre-school and romps through an intense and hyped competition to gain access to a top college, to the potential detriment of young people who may fail to develop an internal compass.

> The fact remains that there is something very different about growing up today. Some students and families are suffering from the frenetic pace, while others may be coping but are enjoying their lives less than they would like. Even those who are doing extraordinarily well, the 'happy warriors' of today's ultra-competitive landscape, are in danger of emerging perhaps a bit less human as they try to keep up with what may be increasingly unrealistic expectations.

A number of students and parents might recognize a pattern in someone they know of what might be described as status anxiety. It begins with the blinders-on competition for the best pre-school, and a vision of the best prep school, the Ivy League name, the best house in the best neighborhood, the "looks good on paper" spouse, and a lucrative career that is accompanied by the ability to purchase all the requisite "toys." Then, somewhere along the road, it hits. That person you might know stops to ask: "Is this what I *want* to do with my life? Is this what I'm *meant* to do with my life? Who am I, anyway, and why didn't anyone ask me that question before, like when I was 18 and before I went to college?"

The recommendation in "Time Out or Burn Out" is: "Let us hope that more of them will take some sort of time-out before burn-out becomes the hallmark of their generation."

Princeton, Brown, MIT, Tufts, Swarthmore, Middlebury, and the University of North Carolina at Chapel Hill are among a growing list of United States colleges and universities that also see benefit in a gap experience, and encourage it (or don't discourage it) as an option for students who are interested. The sense is that students who experience the real world and grow in self-awareness perhaps have a greater maturity, an interest in making the most out of education, and are more well-rounded contributors to their college community.

In February 2008, Princeton University announced plans to establish a "bridge year" or gap year option for 10 percent of incoming freshmen. The announcement made headlines in *The New York Times* and *The Wall Street Journal.*

Another step in growth of gap year options in America is the establishment of AmeriCorps which significantly expands opportunities for students from diverse socioeconomic backgrounds. In 1993, President Bill Clinton signed the bipartisan National and Community Service Trust Act that established AmeriCorps, among other provisions. The program offers individuals the opportunity to serve in communities primarily across the U.S. through a network of partnerships with not-for-profit organizations. In exchange for service, eligible participants receive an education award that can help pay for college. In 2013, the award was $5,500 and there are dozens of colleges that will match the reward and/or offer college credit in recognition of the value of service.

Another evolution designed to grow awareness of an option to going straight to college are USA Gap Year Fairs. These are "a national circuit of events that bring together reputable Gap Year organizations, interested students and parents, high school college counselors and Gap Year experts." They provide students and parents with the opportunity to explore gap year programs. Over five years, the annual fairs have grown from seven events to more than thirty.

In 2012, Ethan Knight left Carpe Diem Education (a gap year program he founded) to start the American Gap Association to support and grow the field. Its primary goal is to focus on accrediting programs and it also intends to advocate for gap years through creating "best practices," providing resources for stakeholders, and other initiatives.

There is a student-led movement among gap alums that is centered at the University of North Carolina at Chapel Hill (UNC). The University's gap year group – GAPPL – has begun an effort to reach out to students across the United States. The group's long-term goal is to legitimize the presence of a gap year in the American education system. Through establishing connections with a variety of students and schools, GAPPL hopes to create gap year fellowships similar to UNC's Global Gap Year Fellowships and Princeton's Bridge Year. They also hope to make parents and schools more receptive to gap years.

Gap Year, American Style Research

As educators and researchers curious about ways that young people grow into adulthood, we began to survey alums about their perceptions of how time out of a formal education path changed them (if at all). An online survey was taken by 300 gap year alums and we conducted more than sixty structured follow-up interviews with students and parents.

Given the strict parameters associated with social science research, we recognize the limits of our study as far as the ability to draw only provisional conclusions at this time. Those that chose to participate in our online survey and interviews, for example, self-selected. So we offer findings in the hope that there will be a much broader range of researching, exploring, and documenting the road traveled by gap students. If you are interested in more information about the survey or research, please contact us. (Our contact information is provided in the "About the Authors" section at the end of the book.)

Research Partners

We sought to include among the potential respondents to the survey a broad representation of gap year participants. Partners provided access to databases of gap year alums, without which the survey would not have been possible. These partners, a mix of gap year consultants and programs, include: the Center for Interim Programs, LLC; City Year, Inc.; Collegeology; Dynamy; LEAPNOW; Student Extended Experiences Consulting, Inc.; and Dr. Monica Andrews. Howard, Merrell & Partners (a full-service advertising agency located in Raleigh, North Carolina) provided invaluable assistance in developing and administering the online survey. SHL Group Ltd. (a global firm specializing in workforce assessments) contributed secondary analysis of data that helped provide a cross-country comparison of the influence of gap years. There are more details about the partners in the Appendix.

About Upcoming Chapters

Through the survey and interviews, we explored the impact of gap years on areas including education, financial awareness, work and careers, community service, global citizenship, and self-awareness. The findings and reflections are offered in the chapters ahead.

In the next chapter on "Journeys in Time," we explore how students arrive at a gap year decision and decide on what to do during a gap year. We follow students on a variety of gap treks and listen to their reflections, including how they may grow through adversity. In this section, gappers also recall the challenges of reverse culture shock that many experience after time away.

In "Education and Learning," gappers answer the question that many parents are most concerned about: Do their sons or daughters enter, or return to college after taking time off? (Hint! Based on those we connected with, most parents don't need to be concerned if this question is weighing on their minds.) We also are interested in gappers' attitudes toward education and learning once they are back in school. In the chapter, gap alums describe whether they have developed skills that help with college life and whether gapping has an impact on academic direction.

In "Gap Year Dollars and Sense," we look at the practical cost of time off experiences: How much does a gap year cost, particularly relative to equivalent time in school? There is perhaps a more important question for students and parents: "Is this investment of time and resources worth it?" In addressing this question, the chapter looks at whether time away from home during a gap year and frequently fending for oneself can lead to any change in financial responsibility.

The next chapter on "Gappers in the Workplace" explores whether real-world experiences on the path through education can impact a career direction. It looks at whether gappers develop the knowledge and skills that can be valued by employers and contribute to success on the job. To anchor this area, we look to researchers in the UK who have investigated whether the knowledge and skills that young people from their country develop similarly and whether these competencies translate into any advantage in landing a job. Finally, we are interested in whether gappers are more or less satisfied in their careers (compared to their peers) and sources of career satisfaction.

"Gap Year Volunteering and Service" considers one of the more popular elements of many gap years – participating in service activities in the U.S. or abroad. In this chapter, we explore whether gap year service experiences translate into a persistent integration of this value and practice into adulthood.

Many view global citizenship as a worthy goal for youth in today's world. In "Global Citizenship: At Home in the World and Seeing Home through the Eyes of Others," we look particularly at those in our survey and interviews who went abroad as part of their gap year. We consider whether their attitudes toward other cultures, people, and religions changed as a result. We also ask whether gappers are influenced by the perspectives of America and Americans they encountered while abroad. A theme that emerges is the difference between being a tourist and being fully immersed in another culture.

The most prominent impact of a gap year, according to what gap alums have told us, is developing a greater sense of self. For "Gappers Look in the Mirror," we ask students (and their parents) to describe how they evolve as a result of their experiences. We also ask gappers (and their parents) what advice they would offer to others considering the option.

Throughout, we have included tips and resources for those interested in a gap year option.

******

It is the hope that this information – and particularly the stories of gap alums – will help frame gap years, as they are beginning to be seen in the United States, as one means through which young people might benefit in educational, financial, and employment terms. Additionally, we hope that the findings will help make the case that service, both here and abroad, can strengthen the bonds of citizenship, including global citizenship. The gap year research also is designed as a first step to inspire broader study by social science researchers as well as those interested in education reform and paths through emerging adulthood.

We also hope that, through the examples of the gappers featured in these pages, there may emerge a sense of the potential of the gap year experience to lead to self-awareness among young adults. The stories and reflections in their own words of those who ventured off the traditional educational track to explore another path may also inspire more students and parents to consider the option of a gap year, American style.

Chapter Two

JOURNEYS IN TIME

"The gap year changed my life, and it changed who I am and what I find important. I did not 'find myself,' because I never considered myself lost. I was given the opportunity to remove myself from my usual patterns, find the morals and characteristics I value about myself, and become the person I wanted to be."

– Will Kimmel

When Emma Impink reflects on her experiences during a gap year far away from home, she thinks about the notion of time.

> One thing that I have to say is that my concept of time changed when I was in South Africa, especially at the baboon place. Days and weeks started taking on huge weight, so much happens in one day and one week, so that a year seems like an enormous amount of time in which huge, huge changes can occur. And then I come home and it's like, 'Oh a semester of college is no big deal.' College is four years. It doesn't seem that long, but the thought of having to be away from especially these baboons who I really, really cared for and had a relationship with, the thought of having to be away from them for a year and go to school is

tough just because so much changes. ... My mom was like 'Oh, you'll be able to go back in a couple of years.' She just doesn't understand that a 'couple of years' now has different meaning than it does to her just because time is different in different places.

Like many other gappers we interviewed, Emma came back from her journey a changed person in some respects. What was once familiar to her took on a strange aura after her experience of living in South Africa. In her case, time took on a sense of weight when she returned. Working closely with primates in a rehabilitation center led to development of a closeness and bonding with them that few can relate to. That is, if they have not had the opportunity, at a relatively early age, to be on a journey through which there can be tremendous growth.

The sense of time for those on a gap year can be in stark contrast to what they experienced in the first eighteen or so years of life, and to what many of their counterparts are experiencing in traditional college environments. High school students' schedules can be programmed with a massive web of classes, extra-curricular activities, and planned experiences. The well-intentioned goal is to help them grow into what many perceive as American success stories, including getting accepted to college.

Why Do I Want to Go to College?

The question of where they will attend college looms large for students and parents. It also looms large for counselors and educators who may be assessed by the number of seniors who go directly to college and the names of the institutions they will attend. Some students click along like metronomes responding to others' expectations. In some cases, they feel the need to take a deep breath, sit back, and ask a different question: "*Why* do I want to go to college now?"

In our survey, the majority (almost 80 percent) asked the "why" question before they arrived on a college campus. Others (20 percent) were on campus in orientation or well into their freshman or sophomore year when they considered the question. A number of those we interviewed described hearing an inner voice cautioning that they may be wasting their time and their parents' (or their own) money because they were not ready to take advantage of the experience. When they learned about a gap year option, it could have come from a number of different sources. For most participants in our survey, the idea was their own initiative followed by parents who introduced the gap year option. Other influences included relatives other than parents, school advisors, teachers, and friends.

Once the gap year option appears on the radar screen, it's time to talk. Communication is particularly important between parents and students. The tone can be tentative as one party or the other may be skeptical about a perceived risk of taking a less traditional route than straight through higher education. The primary risk generally is the nagging thought that the student may not return to the path toward college. This is a time to get all the ideas and perceptions out on the table and explore the motivation, goals, and concerns. If there's consensus to pursue a gap year option, they enter a planning stage.

Narrowing Gap Year Options

Eyes can grow wide as students recognize the vast number of options available to them, and the wide variety can be intimidating at first. By carefully mapping a student's interests, passions, preferences, and constraints against options, a list begins to emerge. What are the student's interests? He or she may like being near the water, playing music, sports, community service, traveling, or one of a myriad of other options. He or she may be open to a short-term job, internship, outdoor education course, or service project to get a taste of a gap year experience.

Here are some questions that students and parents may want to think about to narrow down gap year options.

Questions for Students

- If you could do anything for a year, what would it be? (Dream big!)
- What do you enjoy doing? What are you passionate about?
- Would you like to stay in the United States or go to another country?
- Would you like to be in a country where English is the primary language? Or where another language is spoken?
- Would you like to be with a group of students or have some time on your own?
- Are you interested in living with another family?
- Are you interested in challenging yourself? How?
- Which of these types of experiences sound most interesting: community service, studying, traveling, interning or working (choosing more than one works)?

- If the gap experience costs money, how will you contribute?

Questions for Parents

- Are you interested in using a gap year consultant or counseling service to help you guide your student through a gap year? *Note:* They operate similar to college consultants. They work with your child and your family as a partner and generally have extensive knowledge of gap year options. They charge a fee and many say that it's a worthwhile investment.
- If a gap program costs money, how will costs be covered? Have you discussed financial issues openly and constructively with your child?
- Do you or a member of your family have the interest and time to provide logistical support related to planning a gap year?
- Will it make you more comfortable about your child returning to college if he or she is accepted and defers admission?
- What level of structure do you want your child to have during a gap year experience (age-appropriate structure is often recommended for a first experience)?

A broad plan can involve one or a series of experiences, with the goal of college applications (if they haven't already been accepted and deferred) built in. Frequently, the plan begins with a shorter, structured option for the less experienced traveler to help him or her get a foundation for navigating without hands-on support from home. The plan also needs to be flexible because, once on their way, students tend to make choices that follow their individual direction and growth. They begin to fly, not necessarily in a linear direction.

The specific options for what to do during a gap year can be found on Internet sites or through gap year counselors. Some high schools and colleges have good resources to help students identify options that are right for them. The alums we spoke with emphasized the importance of doing upfront research to narrow down the best match. Through the experiences of gap alums, dozens of options are noted in this book.

Gappers we know have:

- helped build houses
- taught school in cities across America
- hiked the Appalachian Trail
- helped with fund-raising for non-profit organizations
- interned in media
- studied languages in Europe
- sailed on tall ships
- worked as farm hands in Australia
- taught in countries around the world
- worked with orphans in Chile
- taken multiple internships
- attended classes at Oxford
- worked to help rehabilitate baboons in South Africa
- studied coral reefs in the Pacific
- analyzed plants in the mountains of North Carolina
- participated in outdoor education courses
- taught outdoor education courses
- worked as community leaders
- learned from sled dogs in Alaska
- built guitars

- learned stone-carving and wood working
- helped medical teams in rural Kentucky
- worked on organic farms
- helped rehabilitate penguins
- performed in traveling musicals
- made films
- interned in corporate offices
- volunteered on political campaigns, and
- traveled at home and abroad

This list doesn't begin to scratch the surface. The key is to research, reach out and ask other gappers, and talk to program providers, counselors, and references. PlanetGapYear (www.planetgapyear. com) has a searchable database of programs, among other resources. The Center for Interim Studies, LLC, website (www. interimprograms.com) includes sample gap year programs and scenarios, among other resources.

Logistics

Once at least a first activity or program is decided on, it's time for logistics in which parents generally play at least some role. This includes considering and choosing options for insurance, travel, communicating while away, handling money, medical considerations (if there are any), as well as safety and security considerations. Two great resources for information and advice on these and other areas are the American Gap Association (www.americangap.org) and the Center for Interim Programs, LLC (www.interimprograms.com). Many program sites also have valuable information.

Then the time comes to go out into the world. As the day nears for students to leave, there can be nerves and adrenalin such as those that accompany any life event that involves moving into the unknown. This can be similar to the senses a parent may experience dropping their child off at college but perhaps with more pronounced and mixed emotions.

Once underway, much of the gap year journey, whether it involves travel, study, internships, or volunteer service here or abroad, takes on the spirit of adventure. One reason those we surveyed and interviewed are so susceptible to the power of such experiences may be their youth. Eighty-nine percent of young adults who participated in the survey were between the ages of seventeen and nineteen when they began their gap year, with most (80 percent) taking their gap year between high school and college. Whatever their adventure entailed, these young gappers report a generally positive journey with impacts of gained confidence, a (re)ignited interest in learning, an ethic of serving, and a path to self-discovery.

Individual Journeys

One distinction that comes to mind in considering the nature of a gap year is the difference between *taking a trip* and *being on a journey*. Even if the time away from home involves living in another region of the United States, attempting to relate the specifics of one's experience to others – beyond the places visited and sites seen – can be a challenge. There can be a lot to learn from listening to the accounts of journeys than from merely asking about trip itineraries.

Attending carefully to these accounts, a listener might be able to detect one or more of the following attributes that distinguish between a trip and a journey.

- A trip involves observing while a journey requires doing and engaging.
- Being involved in the lives of others is more important than just taking their pictures.
- Making sense of the imprint of one's experience through stories or reflection is more powerful than exhibiting artifacts to impress others.

Many of the gappers' reflections lead to defining the experience in terms that are timeless and not necessarily culture-bound.

David Lofgren

David Lofgren is one of the 14 percent of those in our survey who were employed for part of their gap year. David's early love of learning was nurtured by the fact that he comes from a family of educators. His experience in high school, however, disillusioned him and his grades suffered as a result. He yearned for a more hands-on, engaged approach instead of the book-bound instruction prescribed in his small-town school in New England. As he approached high school graduation, college counselors were pointing him toward the local community college, an option he respected but did not believe was the best fit for him. With no other obvious alternatives being offered, David decided to take a gap year.

His first experience was working on a tall ship, the *Lady Washington*, which sailed along the West Coast. The voyages of the *Lady Washington* offer passengers an opportunity to learn about sailing as well as about the historic ports of call along the coast. David served in a paid officer's position, working some days for fourteen hours. He describes the experience as mind-numbing at times, but it helped instill a work ethic as well as an abiding sense of financial responsibility. Among the most significant discoveries David made during this initial gap-year voyage was his rekindled connection with learning. He read widely and picked up books on existentialist philosophy and psychology in used book stores at various ports of call. He also initiated an informal, self-taught tutorial on the aesthetics of music.

He had no access to television or radio while on board the *Lady Washington* and learned that it was possible and perhaps even preferable for him to live without American media. This experience also had an impact on his habits to this day. He hardly watches television anymore and when he does, he prefers international news (the BBC) and public radio. His love of learning, his search for the engagement of hands-on experience, and the time for study and reflection in the midst of hard work were brought together for David on his gap year journey. He began to see himself as something other than a consumer or a person who needs to be entertained.

Matt Hendren

The early stages of planning and discovery can be easier when a young person receives the support of his or her parents and other influential adults. Matt Hendren is one of the 27 percent in our survey who participated in community service in the United States. He was accepted to colleges in his native state of North Carolina, including the Chapel Hill campus of the University of North Carolina and Davidson College in Davidson, North Carolina. His mother, Catherine Hendren, first heard that Matt was considering a gap year after he attended recruiting weekends at both campuses and returned home less than enthusiastic. "I'm not excited. I'm tired," his mother recalls Matt saying. "And if I'm going to spend your money and four years of my life, I *should* be excited."

Matt was intrigued by the path taken by the wife of one of his high-school teachers; prior to college, she had worked as a volunteer with Mother Teresa in India. She had encouraged Matt to think about "the exceptional things you can do right out of high school." He found that it would be possible for him to get an exceptional experience through service with a program called City Year while doing hands-on work in America's inner-cities. Meeting his parents' main stipulation, that his acceptance to UNC-Chapel Hill be assured by a deferral of his admission to the next school year, Matt found his opportunity for service in inner-city Boston.

Matt painted school buildings early on, later moving into teaching environmental education. He believed that teaching was a more productive option for him than painting and a better match. Through what he describes as the daily grind, Matt lived on a modest stipend provided by City Year. He began to appreciate what it means to live on food stamps and the difficulties of dealing with the basics of life, like transportation, without much spare cash. In retrospect, Matt sees his lack of concern for such daily challenges at the beginning of his gap year as a sign that "he didn't know what he didn't know." Working as a member of a diverse team – diversity is a hallmark of City Year – Matt learned the importance of a positive attitude and that complaining is not a productive strategy. He says that, "My time in Boston helped me set the bar higher for myself, provided me some distance from my friends at home, and let me feel more confident." It taught him that it was possible to shape his own path, a lesson that led him to pursue another year out of school.

As a senior member of the City Year team during a second gap year, he had the opportunity to work in program development, soliciting funds from corporate sponsors. The experience of his second year led Matt to see himself as an entrepreneur, but one working in the area of corporate social responsibility. He also came to see himself as an "outside of the box thinker" in his approach to problem solving, a skill that persisted in his ability to anticipate problems and to persuade others as to viable solutions.

Catherine Hendren observes that after a year in Boston, Matt had learned to listen to his own intuition with greater clarity. When he was offered the job with City Year, he went to the admissions staff at Chapel Hill to request a second deferral. He learned that the University's policy was to grant deferrals for only one year. Catherine anticipated that, as a result, Matt would turn down the City Year offer. Instead, Matt told the admissions staff that, "I'll have to reapply, because I want to serve through City Year." A few months later, he received a letter from the Admissions Office granting him a second year's deferral.

Catherine observes that the gap experience gave Matt the clarity of thought and confidence that he could choose his direction in the face of uncertainty. "You've got to make your own path," she says, "even if it's not what others may see as the right path." She says Matt found his way – "He learned it, loved it, and shares it." And, as will become more obvious in the chapter on volunteering, Matt's journey and clarity on the value of service have illuminated the gap year paths for others.

Cristina Harris

Cristina Harris's journey includes travel overseas. She is among the 41 percent who included this option in her gap year. Her story begins with the intuition at age sixteen that somehow, sometime she would end up going backpacking. As a performer and composer of "introspective piano pop," she has never seen herself bound by any limitations, including the expectation that she go to college immediately after high school. She felt, instead, that she needed a year to gain a better perspective.

True to her intuition, her first adventure, sponsored by San Francisco State University, was backpacking in the Utah desert. Although she found it hard to be away from home in the first couple of weeks, she had just the support she needed from her dad who said that "it was the perfect thing for her to experience, that it was just part of growing up."

After investing time back home working to raise money in order to spend five months in Italy, Cristina was off on a very different experience – one that helped her understand the perspective others had of the United States. Even though she found it difficult, at times, to bear up under criticism of America she heard in Italy, she discovered that traveling leads to learning about how people you meet abroad can be different. Her goal of gaining some distance from her life at home was realized in these kinds of experiences.

Cristina recommends, based on her experience in Italy, that parents and gappers develop an understanding around frequency and mode of communication – a recommendation we heard often. Gappers and parents tell us that communication patterns can vary during a gap year. A number of students, like Cristina, feel a need to be "away when they're away." They are in touch less often than their parents would like, a pattern that can leave moms and dads feeling anxious unless there's an upfront understanding about communication. A number of students write in-depth emails or blogs chronicling their journey that they forward to a list of family and friends. Some students email and call frequently sharing details about their experiences.

Amanda Nooter

Amanda Nooter is one who emailed early and often to keep her parents updated on her gap year and her sense of living in the moment in India. Her mother, Elissa Free, had learned about the gap year concept through friends who are English and thought it was a wonderful idea. After applying early decision and being accepted at Grinnell College in Iowa, Amanda began planning her year with the help of Joanna Lasarek, an associate with the Center for Interim Studies, LLC. Elissa says it was a little scary to send her only child half-way across the world to India, where Amanda participated through the Where There Be Dragons organization.

Through Amanda's frequent communications, Elissa and her husband felt like they were experiencing a gap year vicariously. "We almost felt like we got to do a gap year ourselves, with skyping and photos, emails and blogging, we felt almost like we were there. It was really fun and we were fully engaged." Elissa also sensed Amanda's development over time through the emails. "The first ones were about impressions of places and other people. She reflected more thoughtfully as time went on and began to incorporate more philosophical things in the emails."

Elissa was particularly touched by a piece that Amanda wrote that referred back in time to similar experiences her grandmother, Ann Cottrell Free, as a young reporter in India had observed two generations ago. Here's what Amanda wrote about one of her walks along the Ganges River where she found herself watching a funeral ritual. The ritual involves burning deceased bodies on ghats, or stair-like structures, which are located near a river or water source, allowing ashes from a cremation to be washed away.

> The other day I had a particularly memorable Ganga walk. As I started to make my way from Assi ghat a chorus of "Flowers, madame?" and "Boat, madame?" followed me so I kept turning away saying "nahi, nahi." A troop of little girls and boys came up to me and asked, "What country you from?

What is your name?" I tried practicing a little bit of Hindi with them and they giggled when I made mistakes and looked confused by their frenzied babbling. When the children finally dispersed, a guy who looked like he was in his early twenties, named Kashi, approached me and struck up a conversation. I didn't get creepy vibes from him so I let him walk me all the way to the first burning ghat. He explained how the burning rituals work and which types of people are not burned but rather just dumped in the Ganga. I learned a lot from him and then he left, thanking me for allowing him to practice his English. For a while I just sat at the ghat, watching bodies burn on the giant pyres that are right next to the water. It was surreal to think that I was looking at actual people who were once mothers, fathers, daughters, sons, brothers, and sisters. It made me think of a letter written by my grandmother who had spent some time in India in her youth. In her letter she talked about watching someone's face burn at one of the ghats in Calcutta and how it affected her. There I was, having a very similar experience two generations later.

Elissa says she realized how much her daughter had grown comfortable in another culture when she and her husband had the opportunity to visit Amanda in India. "I was overwhelmed by India and there was a sense of role reversal. She was the parent and I was the child as she led us through a chaotic environment."

When she returned home to Washington, D.C. in the winter before heading to another gap experience in Greece, Amanda says that she was kind of shocked by how everything seemed to have stayed the same as when she left. "I had changed so much and done so much in that same timeframe." Amanda says she tended to live more in the moment after she returned. "I think of life as less scheduled now. Instead of breakfast, lunch, and dinner, I tend to eat when I'm hungry. Days feel longer, I can accomplish more." She adds that she feels differently after the gap experience. "Instead of getting caught up in things, I feel like I have a better and bigger perspective. I can handle things and am more focused on what I want to do. I feel happier."

******

In their work, *Metaphors We Live By*, linguist George Lakoff and philosopher Mark Johnson point to the deep significance of the language we use to convey basic concepts of our experience. One of the concepts that they analyze in depth is that of the JOURNEY. (Their practice of capitalizing metaphors underscores the extent to which they find everyday language linked to the concepts we use to understand the world around us.)

There are versions of the journey metaphor in gap year discussions, when students and parents say that one of their biggest fears is getting off track. Note the competitive and circular nature of the metaphor. Parents also are concerned that their son or daughter, by taking a gap year, may fall behind peers, have trouble getting back on track, or maybe will never return to school. By way of contrast, a telling phrase that gap year alums and their parents use in talking about the gap year option is finding a path, with its more singular direction. In the words of Lakoff and Johnson:

> One thing we know about journeys is that
> JOURNEY DEFINES A PATH.
> A JOURNEY DEFINES A PATH [as in]
> He strayed from the path.
> He's gone off in the wrong direction.
> I'm lost.

The journey metaphor helps to explore the depths of the gap year experience, especially in terms such as Amanda's, that are used to explain its impact on one's self as a person and the surrounding world. In our survey, about one-third participated in academic study abroad.

Oxford Tutorial College

One of the many available academic destinations during a gap year is Oxford Tutorial College or OTC. Oxford Tutorial College specializes in preparing UK students to take their 'A' level exams, a pre-requisite for going on to higher education at a British university. About 20 percent of students at OTC are international. Classes are taught in small seminar-style groups where students are encouraged to develop close relationships with their tutors with the goal of thinking independently and developing academic self-discipline. According to the school's website, "The tutorial method of teaching aims to induce self-belief and confidence in each student and tutors also endeavor to make the work approachable and enjoyable." In the estimate of gappers we have interviewed, the atmosphere of Oxford, the opportunities to do home stays with local families in the UK, and the one-on-one tutor relationships combine for a positive learning experience.

Jon Teel

Jon Teel was one of several alums in our survey who attended OTC as part of their gap year. After being wait-listed at the college of his choice, he and his family decided that a gap year could be beneficial. He looked for an option that would allow him "to build character, study something that interested me, and experience different cultures." His family had traveled overseas and had sponsored foreign exchange students over the years. Jon desired to have a similar experience. He thought that it would help him to become an even better candidate for college and a better person in general.

At OTC, Jon took a European history class and a SAT prep course in which he studied both math and English. He stayed with a host family and traveled in the region. Later he participated in the Wildlands Studies Program in Hawaii, a contrast to the academic halls of Oxford. Wildlands Studies organizes participants in study teams that investigate environmental issues in a hands-on setting. Students can earn college credit for participating in these field projects. Then he spent the last few months of his gap year in San Miguel de Allende, Mexico, where he lived with a host family, practiced his Spanish, and took a painting class. In reflecting on his experience, Jon concludes:

> My motivation to learn, study, and pursue a college education was expanded and defined by my gap year. I had a better sense of what interested me, was excited to share my experience with others, and felt more mature or, at least, more prepared for the challenges of academics.

ITHAKA

ITHAKA is another gap program that embodies a number of characteristics typically associated with academic study-abroad experiences. Although founder Nick Germanacos closed the program in 2003, its alums credit it with guiding their personal and professional development. In its original design, ITHAKA was a residential program based in western Crete off of Greece. It was intended to serve the needs of primarily American students by providing grounding in the Greek culture through academic study and work on local village farms or in native households.

Nick's insistence on academic study, and the mastery of study skills (such as taking notes) and journal writing proved instrumental to the academic success of ITHAKA participants. The etymological connection between being on a *journey* and keeping a *journal* was not lost on Nick and his students.

Nick's gappers were mostly fresh from American high schools and limited in number to groups of twelve to fourteen for each session. Two such clients were Charlotte Smith (now Supple) and Gerrit Lansing. Immersing themselves in the rural culture of Crete, students like Charlotte and Gerrit embody some of ITHAKA's learning in what they gained on their respective journeys.

Charlotte Smith

Charlotte went to ITHAKA after graduating early from her high school. Recalling the impact of the program on her academic pursuits, she said that Nick "pushed us to read and study in a new way. ... He offered me a new approach to learning, which I carried through college and after graduation," including into work experiences. She points out that Nick discouraged students from pursuing college credit for the studies in the program. This approach enabled her to focus on getting as much as she could from the experience without worrying about what grade she would receive. When asked about what she learned about other communities, people, religions, or ways of living, Charlotte responds that the experience made her more culturally aware and contributed to her ability to think critically about the differences among cultures. She adds:

> I learned an incredible amount from an anthropological standpoint. In addition to classes, we each had a job in the community that varied from the local bakery to the sheep herder in the mountains. My job was in a Greek home where I worked with a mom and her kids around the house. I had a

great opportunity to improve my Greek and learn about her family and daily life. There are certainly things that I learned from her that I would not have learned in class. In every sense, I learned a lot about how to observe other people, religions, etc., with an open and inquisitive mind.

Charlotte went on to major in anthropology at Northwestern University. In part because of her observations of the traditional female roles in rural Greece, she focused on women's issues. Nick has very distinct memories of his students over the years, many times recalling the Greek names that he gave them – each of which had significance to the students long after the experience. Charlotte's Greek name was "Irini," the Greek word for peace.

Gerrit Lansing

Another student we interviewed is Gerrit Lansing or "Achilles" as he was known at ITHAKA. According to Nick, Gerrit is a premier example of gappers who had a preconceived notion of what his future held in very traditional, American terms. He was headed to a career in business, with an MBA as his eventual academic goal. Among the many contributions the program made to Gerrit's academic skills, he discovered reading with a purpose (versus reading to satisfy a class assignment) while away and he was always writing. Since leaving ITHAKA he has a habit of carrying a notebook with him everywhere to record his thoughts and observations. But principally he discovered a love of learning and a passion for the Greek classical literature. He also found that, once he committed himself to studying, the appeal of ancient writing was addictive. He sensed, as a result of his ITHAKA experience, that he had more control over things, more of a life direction, and an opportunity to re-orient himself.

Gerrit also grew personally from his experience as a manual laborer on a local farm and by becoming immersed in rural Greek village life. He says he became his own man and discovered a sense of freedom. And he realized from the discovery, both by his exposure to the classics and from his experience as a farm laborer, that "I didn't know that I didn't know myself."

These outcomes led him in the second half of his gap year to the Oxford Tutorial College and the study of classical literature. The combined experience of ITHAKA and OTC provided Gerrit not only with study skills, but it changed his academic life and career goal. Instead of majoring in business, he chose instead to attend the University of the South (Sewanee) and became a classics major with an emphasis in writing. When we first talked with Gerrit, he was considering a career in journalism and possibly an advanced degree in fine arts. When we last checked, he was serving as Digital Director of the National Republican Congressional Committee in Washington, D.C.

Julia Bloch

Seeking to generalize across the sample of our gappers abroad, it is important to keep in mind that these are individual experiences. Julia Bloch's experience is a case in point.

Julia's vision for her gap year journey was spiritual in nature. To gain perspective on her Jewish heritage, she became interested in Buddhism. Her spiritual quest led her to travel as part of a nine-member group via a Pacific Village Institute (PVI)-sponsored trip to India and Nepal. PVI offers cross-cultural learning opportunities in Asia and the U.S. that combine language immersion, home stays, community service, and independent study projects. During her trip she had the opportunity to see and hear the Dalai Lama, visit Tibetan monk monasteries, and stay with a Tibetan family. In a blog posted to the PVI website Julia provides a glimpse of her home stay experience.

At dinner I had super-spicy Sikkimese chillis that look, I mused, like maraschino cherries, and thus have the potential to turn April Fools' Day into Burn Out Your Entire Mouth and Large Intestine Day. I helped her [her home stay mother] with her English 'I already have tea' v. 'I already had tea,' etc. In her notebook she quoted me: 'Everyone wants everyone else's money.' This after I nearly choked on my perfectly halved egg, laughing at pa-la's [her home stay father's] threat to sue me if I played the chilli/cherry joke on him. He had seen some news program in which an American woman sued a restaurant for serving her too-hot coffee. And so I explained, and was later quoted regarding, the American way. Dharamsala [a town in Tibet] is no Ladakh [a region of India] when it comes to the warm, home-y feeling, but eating dinner with my home stay family every night, joking with my ama-la [mother] (why pay for English class when my only fee is dinner?), debating crossover between religion and politics with pa-la...I'm going to miss it here.

Though focused on her spiritual journey during her time in Nepal and India, Julia also was perceptive in her understanding of the impact of American tourists' spending on the local economies. With the ability to pay inflated prices for everyday consumables such as tea, Julia noted that is important to be socially responsible in refusing to participate in a tourist economy that makes goods more expensive for everyone. Globalization in the form of the Western (not just American) tourist is clearly one aspect where gappers would benefit from Julia's insight. It is one thing to study such a concept in the classroom; it is another to understand one's behavior as a contributor to the effects of globalization in the developing world.

Julia summarized her experiences in terms of her growing more culturally fluent. The foundation of this fluency is an awareness that there are other ways of being than what she was used to back home, but that across cultural gaps we can communicate based on what we have in common as human beings. Upon her return to Hamilton College in Clinton, New York, and subsequent transfer to Barnard College in New York City, Julia entered into conversations with delighted Indian cab drivers, adapting Indian cadences the best she could to mirror their language and culture.

Growth Through Adversity

It's easy to fantasize that children never hit bumps in the road and lead lives that are eventful only in a positive sense. However, if we really think about what it takes to grow into confident, resilient, and caring individuals, we recognize that growing through adversity can help lead to maturity. Many gap alums say that working through adversity resulted in a powerful learning experience.

Carly Miller

Carly Miller believes that many gloss over adversity, but shouldn't. "When the going gets rough, you need to figure it out." She found work in Australia through VisitOz, a program that links gappers with jobs on host farms, in vineyards, schools, and in pubs, hotels, and motels. Carly describes her experience as being mostly a cowgirl. "I was working through OZ and the job was to build a barbed wire fence. I failed for two months trying to build that fence. I realized I knew nothing. There was a six year-old girl there who kept telling me to go back to the city. So while I was out there, a ten-year old taught me how to drive a stick shift. A twelve-year-old taught me how to brand cows. And a six-year old challenged me to overcome adversity. Eventually, I figured out how to build the fence and I learned that failure's not scary. It's a chance to learn."

Shoshanna (Shanna) Silverberg

Shoshanna (Shanna) Silverberg did not have a great experience with her high school education and concluded, along with her parents, that she was not ready to go to college. She traveled alone to Ghana to teach at an international school. When she arrived, she was immediately struck by the "adversity all around" and she saw how grinding poverty impacted the lives of those she taught.

A personal challenge that Shanna had to face was being stricken by malaria, in spite of having taken preventative pills prior to and during her trip. After seeking medical evaluation in a local clinic that served her home-stay family, Shanna concluded that she would have to become her own best advocate to find adequate health care treatment. In their weekly phone calls, her parents were remarkably supportive of her seeking treatment in Ghana rather than having her return to the States immediately. She discovered that finding adequate treatment in "the white people's clinic" would require not only her best efforts but substantial financial resources, beyond those available to most around her. This aspect of her journey became an object lesson for Shanna in the role that relative wealth plays in coping with life circumstances.

Viewed from the outside, Shanna's case could be seen as a cautionary tale regarding taking a gap year. But such a conclusion would not do justice to how Shanna and her parents saw this experience as an opportunity to learn from adversity. She learned how to be resourceful and be an advocate for herself. The experience also led her to question what she wanted to dedicate her life to and to examine why it was important to go to school. In her subsequent studies at Hampshire College in Amherst, Massachusetts, she focused on the impact of globalization in the developing world and reflected on how "the American dream thing doesn't connect with the world we live in" and seems to be outdated.

Her journey provided a focus for her college studies. It built a foundation for her job as an advocate for others in the juvenile justice system and as a law student. It also led to deeper introspection through the study of yoga and holistic thinking. From her mother's perspective, the experience spurred her daughter's becoming self-reliant and independent.

Kate Doyne

Kate Doyne's journey took her to Asia and Central/South America as a LEAPNOW program participant. LEAPNOW provides students with access to international and domestic learning experiences that include service and internships. It is "devoted to inner and other exploration and growth." Kate valued the contributions that she and her peers made as Habitat for Humanity volunteers, especially seeing the kids who were going to live in the houses they were building. She also served in a South African orphanage for children whose parents had died from AIDS. But it was her experience in the Peruvian village of Machu Picchu that stands out as a defining moment. After an arduous day of hiking, she collapsed from dehydration and found herself unable to move. She recalls that "the whole village gathered around me after I collapsed and took responsibility for my recovery."

Though not intending to do anything in her travels to put herself in danger, from this experience Kate learned that "vulnerability is not necessarily a shameful thing." She learned that surrendering to fear can rob you from living in the moment. Upon her return home she was compelled to separate herself from former friends whom she perceived to be superficial, wasteful, and generally ungrateful for the comforts all around them – and for whom real adversity had no meaning.

The ways that Carly, Shanna, and Kate dealt with challenges of their respective journeys is yet another imprint that persists beyond the gap year experience itself. And dealing with unexpected, even unwelcome danger, can also be a source of reflection. Reinforcing the journey metaphor in the context of facing challenges, a University of Virginia associate professor of psychology Jonathan Haidt notes in his book, *The Happiness Hypothesis*, that: "Adversity may be necessary for growth because it forces you to stop speeding along the road of life, allowing you to notice the paths that were branching off all along, and to think about where you really want to end up." From all we have heard and seen in the stories of gappers, adversity does jolt them into taking a deep breath and drawing on their physical and mental resources in ways that they may not have on the more traditional path through young adulthood.

Reverse Culture Shock

We have heard from both gap year alums and their parents the difficulties that re-entry after time away from home and their former life can pose for gappers. "Reverse culture shock" is often mentioned and it is a term evoked not just by those who lived abroad. City Year participants also can note the problem that their new perspective creates, after having seen challenges of life in some of America's inner cities.

We've spoken with students who describe their symptoms of reverse culture shock. Examples include:

- being overwhelmed with the lights, sounds, and spaciousness of an American mall;
- recoiling at fast food; or
- preferring to manually wash dishes and clothes rather than depend on modern conveniences such as dishwashers and clothes washers.

What happens that makes (re)adjusting to their former lives difficult? First, it could be the aspect of "being in the present," as one mother puts it. Not being focused on the self as a product to be promoted in the college admissions race (a focus that characterized many of their pre-gap lives) could be another. Seeing adversity not as a threat but as a potentially life-enriching experience could be on the list. Comparing themselves to their high-school or college-age friends often yields insights to how much their experience sets them apart. They may be uncomfortable (re)acclimating to what can appear as a superficial and overly-protective atmosphere of their respective communities or dorm life. The experience of time itself, the speed with which life moves, and a commercialized, comfort-driven culture can stand in stark contrast to the simplicity of cultures where families live in the same room and, though relatively poor, can be rich in their respect for each other and their hospitality toward strangers.

Will Kimmell

Will Kimmell experienced strong reverse culture shock after returning from South America. He spent his first gap semester with Carpe Diem, a program that provides "three-month and yearlong international gap year and study abroad programs focused on community, cultural immersion, volunteerism, and adventure travel."

Will's group volunteered in multiple locations, including at a school in the Amazon where they were hosted by the Machi Ganga tribe. Will describes what it was like when his group was invited to the tribe's celebration of the first day of spring.

> In order to have enough fish, we collected a poisonous root, drugged a section of the water with the juices from the root, and waited for the fish to swim to the surface disoriented. We spent the next two hours swimming out with machetes and clubs to kill the fish and then brought them back to shore. Eventually huge, six-foot long catfish came to the top and the tribesman attacked these fish with arrows, harpoons, and machetes. This was the best day of my life!

He explains how difficult the culture shock was for him and his family when he returned home.

> After living out of a backpack for over three months and living with people who did not rely on much, I was disgusted and embarrassed by my unnecessary wealth. The abundance of stuff I owned literally made me feel ill. I got rid of most of my clothes, I took out everything unessential to living, and I put up a hammock in place of my bed. My parents did not completely support me because they did not want me to get rid of anything I would miss.

Will's additional experiences included working at a penguin reserve in South Africa ("apparently nine hours a day plus biting, smelly birds is a recipe for a great time") and conservation work on a game reserve. He had to readjust to how much his experiences accelerated his growth into adulthood in contrast to the perception of him at home.

> I had worked with peers who were decades older than me. I was an adult, and lived like an adult, and made the mental transition to considering myself an adult. The hardest part of coming home after that experience was that older people (teachers, parents, police, etc.) did not trust me, and treated me like a child. …It is the same at college with a few teachers and staff members. I have lived, worked, and traveled through three different countries in the last year, and now I am a child once again. I am still trying to adjust and adapt the lessons I learned abroad into life here. The gap year changed my life, and it changed who I am and what I find important. I did not 'find myself,' because I never considered myself lost. I was given the opportunity to remove myself from my usual patterns, find the morals and characteristics I value about myself, and become the person I wanted to be.

Transitioning Voices

Julia Bloch's transition back to American mainstream culture reflects those of many gap year wanderers. Once back home, Julia said she wanted to share her experiences but felt like she had a secret that she couldn't adequately explain to those closest to her. Her mother and sister, tiring of her incessant references to her time abroad, frequently asked each other jokingly, "Can we send her back?" She found it difficult to go the super market and be in the midst of American commercialism, after the highs she experienced in India and Nepal. In her attempt to hang on to the experience, she recalls the memory of the audience with the Dalai Lama and savors the entries in her journal where she recorded that, in feeling his joy, "I laughed when he laughed."

Julia's mom, Deborah, looks at the gap year experience as her daughter's chance to reinvent herself. Underscoring what we have heard from other gap year parents, Deborah concludes that the gap year journeys provided her, as a parent, with the opportunity to "learn about my child and celebrate that learning."

Cristina Harris's growing fluency in Italian when she was in Europe and her progress toward discovering her comfort zone abroad made it difficult for her to return to the United States. She found it difficult to adjust to the once-familiar patterns of home: she had come to see the value, for instance, of eating organic foods, drinking socially and in moderation. She quickly discovered that, during social occasions back home, she could establish rapport with the oldest person at the party, with those who had been on similar journeys, and those who could relate to the richness of her experience. Her journey did live on in the stories that she told, in the spirit of oral tradition, to "keep people interested"– and to keep alive, no doubt, the melody of her memories.

Reflecting on the impact of his gap year journey, David Lofgren yearns for the benefits of being able to connect with others who have had similar experiences. Such connections were hard to find among his hometown circle of friends, again representative of what we have heard from many gap year alums. There is something about their journeys that is hard to convey or comprehend if one has not shared a similar experience – or if the listener is not attuned to the journey's deeper meaning.

Hoping to encourage his school to be open to similar options for future students, with the support of his educator parents,

David returned to his high school as a gap year advocate. He and his parents felt that they would likely "create an outcry" in the community because their support for students' taking gap years might be seen as a diversion from the school's goal of maximizing college attendance.

Such may always be the case for those who take the road less traveled. Journeys of this sort may by their very nature be exceptional, not for the timid. It may also be a comment on the nature of high school education in the U.S. that counselors and parents tend to see acceptance to college as a student's only path to their success. This is not always the case, as David's example proves, when he found that he could travel as a result of his gap year to a four-year college with the aid of his internal compass.

******

A thread in the interviews we have had, variously expressed, is that gappers want to hold on to the essence of their journeys. They are looking for how to recapture and preserve the feelings and the senses of where their travels took them – to "smell the smells, see the colors, and hear the prayer calls," in the words of Roberto Latino, a gap year intern in Istanbul. They seek to preserve the insights and the relationships of their experiences in ways that often prove inadequate to the demands of getting back on track, and returning to school.

Will Kimmel developed the habit of writing in a journal every day during his time in South America and South Africa as an integral part of processing and reflecting on his experiences. He is still impacted by an incident that occurred on his way back to the United States.

On the flight home, my journal was stolen in the Guatemalan airport, and I am still distraught by the loss. It was my only real connection to the emotions and thoughts I had during the trip. I experienced so many things every day that there is no way I will be able to remember everything I did. I cannot track the affects the trip had on my personality or spirituality, and I do not know how I changed over time. Nothing I brought back was equal to the value I placed in that book.

Emma Impink, whose journey to South Africa led to a different perspective on time, speaks for many others when she says:

It's been a little bit hard being home. I've been reading a lot of travel books, just travel journals of people, and I've found that they never write that chapter. They always end 'and now I'm home.' And they never give you that chapter about what it's like to be home, and how it's really hard to come back and that transition period and when you're sort of still craving seeing the people who you saw all the time. So it's become for me how can I keep the way that I felt and those people and those experiences a part of my daily life and a part of hopefully something I can do in the future.

When we ask students and parents to describe a gap year, the term that frequently pops out is that it's perceived as a "transformational" experience. The dictionary definition of the term relates to undergoing a "profound change in form, appearance, or character from one stage of life to the next." An example provided is the metamorphosis that occurs when a caterpillar transforms into a butterfly. We can't say that gapping means a young American will become a butterfly, but the alums we spoke to attest that they at least emerged from their cocoons after the journey.

******

For the majority of the gappers we've connected with, the next step in their journey includes arriving at college where they continue to absorb the experiences from their time away. We explore what happens when gappers go on to college in the next chapter.

******

Gap Year Survey Findings Summary

- *When did gap alums take a gap year?* The majority of respondents (80 percent) took a gap year before college – 20 percent were in school when they decided to take a gap year.
- *Who came up with the gap year idea?* Most participants said it was their idea followed by parents, relatives other than parents, school advisors, teachers, and friends.

Tips

- *Communicate.* When deciding whether to take a gap year, effective communication at least among parents or guardians and the prospective gapper is important. Invest the time to talk through the reasons for taking a gap year and what is expected as a result (aside from going to college!).
- *Narrow Options.* There are thousands of options when considering what to do during a gap year – "If you can dream it, you can do it!" Students and parents can ask questions about interests, preferences, budgets, and other issues to help narrow the options. (See a suggested list of questions earlier in this chapter.)

- *More Structure at First.* For a first experience, particularly for younger and less seasoned gappers, consider programs with age-appropriate structure. Talk with program staff, ask for references, and talk with program alums and parents.

- *Gap Year Consultants and Counselors.* Consider working with a gap year consultant or counselor in planning the gap year. They charge fees but the vast majority of families who choose to work with them say that their experience, program knowledge, and ongoing support is well worth any expense.

- *Logistics.* Parents likely will play an important role in logistics before and during a gap year (e.g., insurance, travel, communications, handling money, medical planning, safety and security considerations, college application process – if there isn't a deferral).

- *Resources for gap year ideas, planning, and logistics.*
  - American Gap Association (www.americangap.org)
  - Center for Interim Programs, LLC (http://www. interimprograms.com)
  - Planet Gap Year (http://planetgapyear.com)
  - USA Gap Year Fairs (www.gapyearfairs.org)

Chapter Three

LEARNING AND EDUCATION

*"My gap year gave me the confidence and knowledge
to make good decisions and effectively skip many
experiences that I saw my fellow students experiencing. I
was clear about my objectives and intentions for college,
but flexible and just energetic about the opportunity to
spend four years in college."*

– Jon Teel

The answer to the following question might be a surprise. Out of a class of one hundred ninth graders, how many students do you believe will graduate from high school and then graduate from college "on time"? In other words, how many will graduate from twelfth grade, proceed to college, and then earn a degree in four years?

If the answer was 40 percent, 50 percent or higher, you are probably on track with what many Americans would say. If the past assessments are an indicator of the future, however, the answer would be off track with what research tells us. According to the National Council of State Legislatures, eighteen of those 100 ninth graders are likely to graduate "on time." *That's 18 percent graduating from high school, moving to college the next fall, and graduating in four years.*

Consider the following:

- Nearly one-third of students don't graduate from high school "on time," according to the Alliance for Excellent Education.
- Of those who go to college, more than 30 percent will drop out during their freshman year, according to the U.S. Department of Education.
- It takes an average of more than six years to graduate from college, according to the National Council of State Legislatures.

Yet the majority of high school students and their parents believe they are headed for completion of an "on time" four-year college education.

The act of entering college, however, isn't necessarily an indicator of earning a degree or of getting the most out of higher education. A more valuable question might be: What will my child get out of going to college (in addition to a piece of paper called a degree, if they meet the requirements)? Instead of *access* to college, should a focus be on *success* in college?

******

In our survey and conversations with gap alums and their parents, we were interested in their view of any relationship between choosing a gap option and what they perceive as success in higher education.

Wes Cannon

Wes Cannon says he was an average student in high school and "not really involved in anything outside of class." Both of his parents had concerns that if Wes had gone straight to college, he would have flunked out or dropped out (and Wes doesn't disagree).

After spending two gap years working on tall ships sailing up and down the East Coast of the United States, Wes recounts:

> I ended up making some drastically different decisions than what I had planned on in high school. The most important result to date would have to be my college performance. In high school, I wanted to go far away from home and my father's college (he is a college teacher). I also wanted to go to a big university and have lots of fun. I chose at the end of my gap years to go to the school my father teaches at, which is a small liberal arts school. While I was there, I designed my own major, became involved in student politics, and became the Student Government Association treasurer and president. I started a rugby club, and helped found a leadership fraternity. As far as grades went, every semester's grades were above my best high school semester, and for a few semesters, I was taking almost a double workload of 24 credit hours.

Wes adds that, "Another side effect was I realized through meeting a lot of people in the real world that it really isn't as important as most kids believe to go to college right away." One of our favorite stories from the interviews we conducted comes from Clare Cannon, mother of Wes. Clare says she was having a conversation with a teacher who taught Wes in an Entrepreneurial Studies class. They were talking about Wes and the teacher said, "I have 19 students in my class who want to get an A. And I have Wes who wants to learn how to start a business." Clare adds that Wes returned from his gap experiences wanting to know "why." She says with tremendous pride that with all of Wes's accomplishments in college and his graduating in four years, "he floored us all."

Stuart Moore

Stuart Moore is one of the 20 percent in our survey whose gap opportunity arose after he accepted and entered college. He enthusiastically arrived for freshman year at Clemson University in South Carolina with the vision of enjoying college life, and a scholarship to help pave the way. Soon, Stuart found he was enjoying college life too much, carousing with his peers four or more nights a week. By the end of his sophomore year, his grades were slipping, his classes felt boring, and he was in danger of losing the scholarship. He was "burned out." Stuart and his father, Tom Moore, describe the beginning of his junior year with the same two words: "a disaster."

Tom was familiar with the gap year concept and suggested that Stuart's taking time away from school might be the remedy for his academic challenges. Together, father and son outlined a series of gap activities.

Stuart's time off included working as a farm hand with a family friend. He then attended an Outward Bound Outdoor Leadership course. He became certified as a first responder, an ability that equipped Stuart to help search for hikers who were lost or injured in wilderness areas. The Outward Bound course provided Stuart with career-related skills and helped him to gain employment during summers, on campus, and after graduation. It also provided him with the opportunity to face and overcome a fear of heights, when he had to complete a rock climbing course in North Carolina.

Among the important lessons Stuart learned – and continues to apply to this day, according to his father – is that before taking charge and leading a group in the outdoors, "you must master yourself."

Stuart returned to Clemson with more confidence, with skills in time management, and a greater appreciation of his opportunity to learn. He switched majors and his grades improved "exponentially," averaging a 3.8 grade point average (on a 4.0 scale) during his final semester. He gave up his former pattern of partying with other students, and chose to spend less time with television or video games, finding them a distraction from learning.

When asked about the gap year's impact on his personal development, Stuart says that, had he not taken the time off, he would have become "a drastically different person." He would not be as comfortable today meeting people from different walks of life and would be much less determined to persevere in spite of challenges.

He now sees himself as a group leader who is able to work with others to solve problems. He has a clearer sense of direction in what he wants to do with his life. His father sees a young man who became re-engaged intellectually, much more open in sharing his vulnerabilities, and a capable, confident leader.

"I wish my son had encountered the gap-year idea three years earlier," says his father, Tom. "For that matter, I wish I had encountered it forty years ago." A seasoned public policy expert, Capitol Hill veteran, and writer, he has formed a perspective on the value of gap years. Tom allows us to share his written view on the potential impact of taking a break from the traditional classroom.

Today we never stop telling our kids how intelligent they are, how lucky they are to live in such a mobile, technologically advanced, and affluent society. Yet for all its abundance and limitless choices, today's world poses extraordinary challenges to our children. The ancient verities and old certainties are gone, leaving many kids confused, aimless, even self-destructive. The family, cultural, and societal norms that once helped them mature into functional adults have changed radically.

We expect our children to go through twelve intensive years of primary and secondary school and then head off to college, a growing prerequisite for middle-class status and economic security. Yet think for a moment what those twelve years can do to our children. Most kids endure a rigidly prescribed curriculum ladled out to them in regular fifty-minute intervals, during which they must sit obediently and receive knowledge passively, interrupted only by prescribed exams. The result is often a loss of creativity, spontaneity, independent thinking, self-knowledge, and maturity, even if kids do manage to imbibe a degree of academic knowledge.

Enter the gap year. This is the simple yet revolutionary idea that students should take a year off between high school and college, or during college, for a period of self-examination and self-discovery. Gap years have the potential to change the lives of individual young people in profound ways.

Rebecca Krass

Rebecca Krass (friends and family call her Becca) graduated from high school in Palo Alto, California. She was a strong student, although she was less than engaged in high school.

When it came to applying to college, she was confident that she would get accepted at competitive schools and didn't take the application process too seriously. Her parents were confident. Counselors were confident. The time came to compile a list of where to apply. Becky applied to nine schools. Her list included "safety schools" such as the University of California, Los Angeles, and the University of California, Berkeley. The list also included selective schools in the East, including several Ivy League institutions. The assumption was that Becca would have her choice of colleges. The plan was to wait for the fat acceptance envelopes to arrive in April. The family then would take an already-scheduled trip back East to visit the schools Becca had gotten into.

Then came a Tuesday in April when four thin envelopes arrived in the mail. Becca had been turned down by Harvard, Princeton, Duke, and Tufts. Three days later, more thin envelopes arrived. It was time for a change of course.

The college counselor (who had said "This would never happen") suggested Becca consider a gap year and pointed her in the direction of Neil Bull, founder of the Center for Interim Programs, LLC. The new plan was to head East but, instead of college visits, the Krass's would meet with Neil at his office in Cambridge, Massachusetts. Daniel Krass, Becca's dad recalls that they walked away from the first meeting with fresh ideas, a packet of information, and a great relationship with Neil. When Becca graduated from high school, he adds, it was expected by friends and educators that she would go straight to college.

"Her friends were stunned she wasn't going." Instead of college, Becca was headed for a gap year. Her new plan came into focus and, like many gap students, she would combine a group of experiences. She spent time in Costa Rica with a focus on studying leatherneck turtles, worked in Nepal, and sailed with a small group of students during the summer to round out the year.

"She got to see how the rest of the world lives," says Debbie, Becca's mom. "I think the experience sailing, in particular, gave her a lot of time to think about her life. The gap year allowed her the time to mature, to allow change to happen." Becca reapplied to college and was accepted at Dartmouth, Duke, and Williams. In comparing her second set of college applications to her first set, she saw herself pre-gap year as mostly concerned with the trivial. As the result of her gap year, Becca says she was more focused on "why I wanted to go to college." She chose Williams College in Williamstown, Massachusetts, as the best fit.

By the time she got to Williams, says her mom, "She was ready to go. She was refreshed mentally. So psyched about her classes. So psyched about her teachers. She was ready to make something of herself. The result is that she got the maximum value out of the college experience."

Becca's dad recalls a conversation with an administrator from Williams. At that time, 4 percent of Williams students took a year off. The administrator said "one hundred percent of the time when a student takes time off, the student is better off. And the school is better off for the student's investing time off."

Time Out or Burn Out

Wes's, Stuart's, and Becca's journeys from being "blasé" or "burned out" to becoming active and passionate learners characterize the experiences for most of the gap students we interviewed. Their re-energized commitment to learning, discipline, and perseverance, however, does not match the profile of the majority of American students.

A number of today's college students are at risk of what some experts call "meandering" through and around college, if they don't drop out all together. They may try an academic major here or there as they extend the time they spend in college and try to imagine a career.

There is a school of thought that such a meandering pattern through college is not only the norm, it is even desirable. Dr. Jeffrey J. Arnett is a research professor in the Department of Psychology at Clark University in Worcester, Massachusetts. He is credited with coining the term "emerging adulthood" to describe what transpires with young people between the late teens and mid-twenties. Dr. Arnett makes the case in *Emerging Adulthood* that students *should* float around in college, trying out various classes and various majors with a notion of finding out about themselves and what kind of job would fit them. In college, "many are waiting for something to click, searching for that aha moment when they know they have found their true calling. Some find it, some do not. But college at least gives them the opportunity."

The experiences of gap year advocates, alums, and their parents seem to counter Dr. Arnett's meandering formula with the notion that structured time away from school can be an antidote to lack of educational focus. Eva Brann, a former Dean and current tutor at St. John's College (Annapolis), wrote in 1995 about the advantages of students' taking longer to graduate from college as long as there is a plan or structure involved. "While aimless and dawdling wastes time and money, a well-controlled stretching out of the college years ... has several short- and-long term advantages, both pedagogical and practical. The rush to finish is one of a number of ill-conceived notions which this college [St. John's] should oppose as articulately as possible, both for the sake of American students and its own reputation."

Ms. Brann looks to gap years as a positive option for students.

> In that year away students begin to see how their education prepared them for the working world, and they also begin to understand what they need to learn that is not taught in this or any other school. Often they discover what they really want to do (or can't bear doing) after they graduate, and they begin to make the connection that will help them afterwards, perhaps even to the first post-graduate job.

******

In the essay, "Time Out or Burn Out for the Next Generation," admissions officers of Harvard College agree about the potential impact of students' taking time off.

> Regardless of why they took the year off or what they did, students could not be more effusive in their praise. Many talk of their year away as a life-altering experience or a turning point, and most feel that its full value can never be measured and will pay dividends the rest of their lives. Many come to college with new visions of their academic plans, their extracurricular pursuits, the intangibles they hoped to gain in college, and the many career possibilities they observed in their year away. Virtually all would do it again.

The gap survey and interviews included specific questions related to education and learning. As noted earlier, we asked whether students do, in fact, proceed or return to college after a gap experience. We asked about the impact of these experiences on one's attitude toward formal education. We were curious about the individual's performance in college. And we wanted to know about any influence on an academic major or course of study.

Will They Return to College?

It's understandable that the primary questions on the minds of gap parents is, "After a gap year, will my child go to or return to college?" It's embedded in the American dream that a college education is a key to success. Studies show that college graduates earn hundreds of thousands of dollars more in a lifetime than high school graduates. What if the years of preparation, planning, and saving end up with college being postponed for years, or a son or daughter not attending college at all in the foreseeable future?

The majority of the students in our survey returned to college (80 percent within six months and 90 percent within a year). We had the opportunity to talk with a number of students who had not entered or returned to college within a year. Several took an additional gap year before college, for example, when they were offered paid employment opportunities. A few had family challenges, such as death or illness, that required their time and dedication.

When those in our survey did return to school, they attended public, private, and community colleges across the country and a few chose to attend college overseas. A recommendation that we heard from parents, students, and educators is that those intending to pursue a gap experience apply to college and then request a deferral. For many students, this means that the application process is one less item that they need to devote energy to during a gap year. Having their college future assured can be a liberating feeling for students (and their parents). Although students can and do include applying to college as part of their gap year plan (frequently building in time around the holidays and between gap experiences for this purpose), it can be logistically challenging to complete forms when in the midst of a gap year sequence.

About Deferrals

We often are asked about what college officials think about gap year options. Are they in favor of them? One indicator is the policies schools have about deferrals. Based on the experts we have talked to, most colleges will grant a deferral as long as a student offers a description of what they plan to do during time off.

In our survey, 77 percent of respondents applied to college before taking a gap year and 23 percent report that they did not. Of those who applied, 93 percent were accepted to at least one college and 7 percent were not accepted to a college. Regarding deferrals, more than half (56 percent) of respondents requested, and received, a deferral of admission for their gap year and 44 percent did not.

The exact deferral requirements vary from college to college. Boston University, for example, requires a non-refundable deposit along with a "Request for Deferral of Admission" form. The form includes a Personal Statement section that asks: "Please tell us your plans for the period of deferment. Specify travel, work, and educational objectives and relevant dates." The College of Charleston (South Carolina) asks for "a brief statement about your plans during the period of deferment. If you are uncertain, please update us once your plans have been made." Like a number of colleges, the College of Charleston's website also includes a section on gap year options. In a note "To the Parents of Gappers," it states: "For some of you it may be hard to understand why your student would want to take a year or so off from education or from their job. For others you may understand it but do not understand how taking a gap year can be beneficial." The website continues to provide links to "a wealth of information to set you at ease and answer all the questions you have regarding gap years."

Another option for students is to consider whether they would like to earn college credit in exchange for gap experiences. Colorado College, for example, lists gap year options on its website for students that it invites to start their freshmen experience in the winter (it's called the Winter Start program) along with the related number of college credits students might earn.

Parents may also wonder what happens if their child, as a result of their gap year, changes his or her mind about the college that is the best match for them. That happens. Our son, Adam, for example, was headed for Wake Forest University in North Carolina. After taking two gap years, he founded a more solid match for his interest in science at Evergreen State College in Olympia, Washington. If one has deferred and paid a non-refundable deposit, one may risk losing what generally amounts to several hundred dollars. On the other hand, the gapper – and the college – may well be better off due to the more synergistic match between student and institution.

As one admissions officer stated, "I don't know of a college worth their salt that wouldn't welcome a student who took a thought-out gap year to campus because of the value they bring to the community."

Here are the colleges those we connected with attended after a gap year.

Colleges Attended After a Gap Year

Alfred University (New York)	Franklin W. Olin College of Engineering (Massachusetts)
American InterContinental University, London (United Kingdom)	Friends World College (New York)
American University of Rome (Italy)	Furman University (South Carolina)
Antioch College (Ohio)	George Washington University (District of Columbia)
Arizona State University (Arizona)	Georgetown University (District of Columbia)
Art Institute of Pittsburgh (Pennsylvania)	Gettysburg College (Pennsylvania)
Austin Community College (Texas)	Grinnell College (Iowa)
Babson College (Massachusetts)	Guilford College (North Carolina)
Barnard College (New York)	Hamilton College (New York)
Bates College (Maine)	Hampshire College (Massachusetts)
Boston University (Massachusetts)	Harvard University (Massachusetts)
Brandeis University (Massachusetts)	Haverford College (Pennsylvania)
Bryn Mawr College (Pennsylvania)	Hiram College (Ohio)
Bucks County Community College (Pennsylvania)	Hobart College (New York)
Cabrillo College (California)	Indiana University (Indiana)
Calvin College (Michigan)	Ithaca College (Ithaca)
Carleton College (Minnesota)	Johns Hopkins University (Maryland)
Cecil College (Maryland)	Kalamazoo College (Michigan)
City College of San Francisco (California)	La Universidad Nacional de Costa Rica (Costa Rica)
Clackamas Community College (Oregon)	Lawrence University (New York)
Clark University (Massachusetts)	Long Island University (New York)
Cleveland State University (Ohio)	Macalester College (Minnesota)
Colby College (Maine)	Marlboro College (Vermont)
College of Charleston (South Carolina)	Massachusetts College of Arts (Massachusetts)
Colorado College (Colorado)	McDaniel College (Maryland)
Cooper Union (New York)	Middlebury College (Vermont)
Cornell University (New York)	Montgomery College (Maryland)
Curry College (Massachusetts)	Mount Holyoke College (Massachusetts)
Cuyahoga Community College (Ohio)	Naropa University (Colorado)
Davidson College (North Carolina)	New School University (New York)
Delaware County Community College (Delaware)	New York University (New York)
Denison University (Ohio)	North Carolina State University (North Carolina)
DePaul University (Illinois)	Northeastern University (Massachusetts)
Dickinson College (Pennsylvania)	Northwestern University (Illinois)
Drexel University (Pennsylvania)	Notre Dame College (Ohio)
Earlham College (Indiana)	Ohio Wesleyan University (Ohio)
Eckerd College (Florida)	Oklahoma City University (Oklahoma)
Elon University (North Carolina)	Pikes Peak Community College (Colorado)
Emerson College (Massachusetts)	Pitzer College (California)
Emory University (Georgia)	Portland State University (Oregon)
Evergreen State University (Washington)	Prescott College (Arizona)
Fort Lewis College (Colorado)	

Colleges Attended After a Gap Year(contd.)	
Princeton University (New Jersey)	University of Colorado, Boulder (Colorado)
Providence College (Rhode Island)	University of Connecticut (Connecticut)
Quinnipiac University (New York)	University of Denver (Colorado)
Rancho Santiago Canyon College (California)	University of Illinois, Chicago (Illinois)
Reed College (Oregon)	University of Iowa (Iowa)
Regis University (Colorado)	University of Maine (Maine)
Rhode Island School of Design (Rhode Island)	University of Mary Washington (Virginia)
Rice University (Texas)	University of Maryland (Maryland)
Rutgers University (New Jersey)	University of Massachusetts, Amherst (Massachusetts)
Saint Joseph's University (Pennsylvania)	University of Massachusetts, Boston (Massachusetts)
Salem State College (Massachusetts)	University of Michigan (Michigan)
San Diego City College (California)	University of New Hampshire (New Hampshire)
San Francisco State University (California)	University of North Carolina, Chapel Hill (North Carolina)
Sarah Lawrence College (New York)	University of North Texas (Texas)
Savannah College of Art and Design (Georgia)	University of Pennsylvania (Pennsylvania)
Simmons College (Massachusetts)	University of the South (Tennessee)
Simon Fraser University (Canada)	University of Southern Maine (Maine)
Skidmore College (New York)	University of Surrey (United Kingdom)
Smith College (Massachusetts)	University of Tennessee, Chattanooga (Tennessee)
Southern Connecticut State University (Connecticut)	University of Vermont (Vermont)
Southern Oregon University (Oregon)	University of Virginia (Virginia)
Southern Vermont College (Vermont)	University of Washington (Washington)
Spartan College of Aeronautics and Technology (Oklahoma)	University of Wisconsin, Madison (Wisconsin)
St. John's College (New Mexico)	Vista Community College (California)
St. Mary's College of Maryland (Maryland)	Washington University at St. Louis (Missouri)
Temple University (Pennsylvania)	Wellesley College (Massachusetts)
Trinity College (Connecticut)	Wesleyan University (Massachusetts)
Tufts University (Massachusetts)	West Chester University (Pennsylvania)
Tulane University (Louisiana)	Western Washington University (Washington)
Union College (Connecticut)	Westfield State College (Massachusetts)
Université Paul Valery (France)	William Smith College (New York)
University of Alabama (Alabama)	Williams College (Massachusetts)
University of Arizona (Arizona)	Yale University (Connecticut)
University of California, Berkeley (California)	
University of California, Santa Cruz (California)	

Access to vs. Success in College

We've suggested that parents (and students) who are primarily focused on access to college right after high school may be missing a more important question. Rather than focusing on access, should the focus be on how to define success during and after college?

71

One definition of success in college may be graduating "on time" or in four years. In the survey, 82 percent reported that they graduated in four years or less, after we factored out those still in school. Fourteen percent reported they graduated in five years and 4 percent in six years.

If you compare this with the national average of graduating in six years, parents and students may note that graduating "on time" might result in cost savings of college tuition. It can be argued that the graduation rates for many of the schools that the students returned to after time off are higher than the national average. However, based on the interviews with gap students, a main reason for graduating in four years or less is that they are more focused and passionate about education and learning after taking a break. Gap students also have experienced life outside of an academic circle and may not be hesitant about – or even look forward to – life beyond college.

Another marker of college success can be what students learn in college. The gap year alums responded that, returning to school, they were much more interested in education than their peers. Many gained a better understanding of issues that interested them, often leading to a major in college that otherwise they would have not pursued. A gap year gave them the ability to get off the treadmill, to focus on themselves, and to ignite or reignite a passion for learning. For many students, the ability to draw connections between education and "real world" lessons made a difference.

Julie Siwicky

Julie Siwicky spent the first part of her gap year in India with a group sponsored by Global Learning Across Borders (GLAB). The second half she spent in New Zealand as a teaching assistant in an elementary school. Because of these experiences, she says: "I'm more interested in pursuing my education in the sense that I better understand its value in the real world. I can better identify if/how material that I study will apply to my life outside of college. For example, my econometrics class (math, statistics) would probably carry very, very little importance for me if I had not taken a gap year. Now, I see that the tools that it gives me will be super-useful when I want to contribute to the field of economics, post-college. I feel like I'm way more motivated to learn the material than I would be without having taken a gap year."

Erin O'Neil

Erin O'Neil – whose gap year included time in Hawaii, Fiji, Central America, and Europe – also testifies to the positive impact of being able to connect education with real-world experiences, making her a more valuable member of the college community.

> My experiences made me eager to pursue my education. I felt empowered after learning about the world in a different way. I felt as though I was bringing a unique perspective and set of experiences to my classes, making me a more valuable asset to my college than I would have been before. I found that so many of my experiences connected with what I was learning. Perhaps I sought out classes where that would happen, but at the very least, my experiences gave me direction in what I wanted to pursue. I sought out classes that had to do with global issues and the environment, such as courses in natural disasters, Latin American coups, environmental sociology, epidemics in history, etc.

The skills and knowledge that Erin gained from her gap year experiences also emboldened her to apply for an on-campus research project as a freshman at Tulane University in New Orleans – something she says she could not have seen herself doing without her gap year experience.

> After my gap year, I really believed in myself both academically and socially. My freshman year of college, I was given the opportunity in my environmental sociology class to participate in an extra two-credit research project. The professor wanted four or five students to work with him doing research on how an oil refinery was affecting residents of a small town nearby. The project involved a lot of self-starter work and communication with residents. Having performed marine biology research and dealing with strangers on a grassroots level during my gap year, I jumped at the opportunity, when I normally would have been frightened and passed it up. I wound up loving the research project and was an integral part of its success, helping develop survey questions and surveying the residents of the town to help compile a database to present at a town meeting to raise awareness and start a grassroots movement in the community to stop the pollution, which was causing illness.

******

In interviews, many gappers credited their time away from academia with their developing the ability to make better and more informed decisions for themselves, including about where to go to college and their attitude toward learning. This ability, in turn, resulted in greater "ownership" of their education.

When *does* a young person on the road to college have the opportunity to build decision-making muscles? Of course, they are faced with decisions every day. The decision can seem small (what should I eat? do I go to the mall or tackle homework?), risky (do I do what my friends are doing, or walk away?), or profound (what kind of person do I want to be and what values do I stand for?). The decision can even be whether or where to attend college. For most, there's a stream of well-intentioned advisors to help guide their decisions – parents and other relatives, peers, teachers, and counselors.

For gappers, being outside of their "comfort zone" and facing unfamiliar challenges can lead to a growth in decision making ability, and their ability to make more grounded choices about their educational path.

Megan Kelly

Megan Kelly applied to ten colleges and got into only one that she "did not like to begin with." Opting for a gap year, she attended Oxford Tutorial College in England where she took writing classes ("I use the exercises and advice still") and a philosophy class. She also traveled in New Zealand. She says that, "I returned to the States after deciding to not attend university in the UK, I was more aware of my choices then I had been. I was making *certain decisions* [our emphasis] about my education that I had not even thought about during high school. I was able to look ahead and plan for that future because I had more information about the world and myself."

When we last heard from Megan, she was a senior at Emerson College in Boston. She says she thinks about her time abroad almost every day. "When you travel alone or are within a program, the ability to think on your feet, being flexible about everything, and living and working well with others is acquired and strengthened. It was a daily thing and something I use today."

Bathsheba Demuth

Bathsheba Demuth pursued a gap year because she wasn't feeling excited about college, and wanted some real-life experience before pursuing academics again. "I thought that college, since it's a big commitment of time and money, is something that one should be very enthusiastic about and dedicated to, rather than just something to do after high school."

Her gap experiences took her to Canada. "I ended up spending two years in the small Native American village of Old Crow, Yukon. After three months there I couldn't imagine going anywhere else. Old Crow is a village of about 300 people, eighty miles north of the Arctic Circle, and is accessible only by airplane. I was basically an apprentice to a local Athapaskan family that kept a sled-dog team, so I participated in all aspects of the local culture and ran dogs. After I had been in Old Crow for about six months, I also began teaching GED English and math at the local community college branch."

Bathsheba took another year off to write a book about her time in Old Crow. She credits her experience with getting into the top college on her list.

> I owe my gap time to getting into my college of choice, I'm almost certain of that. I was a good student in high school, so I had the academic background – but the gap year and the fact I did something very self-directed and not a prepackaged sort of program is probably the biggest factor into my acceptance at Brown.

She also addresses those who are concerned that returning to college older (although generally wiser) than peers will have a negative impact.

I think just being older helped considerably. For one thing, I was a lot less susceptible to peer pressure – it was pretty easy to say no to partying or other behaviors I didn't want to engage in. Because I knew I could succeed in a place like the Arctic, I didn't depend on all my sense of self-worth from the opinions of peers. I also had a lot more self-confidence academically, and was better able to articulate what I wanted to study and why. I think professors responded well to this.

When we last heard from Bathsheba, she had graduated from Brown University, had signed with a reputable literary agency, and was working on a United Nations funded project in Eastern Europe that assists victims of human trafficking and women fleeing domestic violence. Bathsheba concludes:

After my gap year I had more ownership over my college experience. I think I learned that *my choices* [our emphasis] made an enormous impact on my educational path and wanted to take advantage of that opportunity. ...I think it made me more focused and mature about how I wanted to spend my time in college. I took the gap year in part because I wasn't feeling excited about higher education, but when I left I was very happy and looking forward to starting college. After taking some time off, college wasn't just that thing you do after high school – it seemed like an *informed choice* [our emphasis]."

Like Megan and Bathsheba, the majority of participants in our survey report that they are not only more passionate about learning, but they take academic work more seriously after a gap year.

Maggie Hureau is a City Year alum who, when we heard from her, was working for City Year where she managed two teams serving in

New York City schools. She attributes her academic achievement in college to her gap year experiences. "It changed my attitude toward learning in general and about what a privilege it is to be able to attend college. It made me incredibly more motivated to go to college and do well. In fact my grades skyrocketed in comparison to high school."

After a gap year, 66 percent of students in our survey report taking academic work more seriously and 24 percent answered they regarded studies "about the same" as before a gap year. Eight percent report their attitude was somewhat less serious after a gap year and 2 percent report taking studies much less seriously.

Although not all of the gap alums grades "skyrocketed" after a gap year as did Maggie Hureau's, the survey participants fared well in terms of academic achievement. Seventy-four percent of our respondents reported earning a grade point average of 3.1 or higher once they returned to college after a gap year. That breaks down to 34 percent earning 3.6 to 4.0 and 40 percent earning between 3.1 and 3.5. Nine percent went to colleges that don't use grades to measure achievement and 2 percent earned between 2.0 and 2.5 for their grade point average.

A *New York Times* article supports the proposition that gap years can contribute to relative higher GPAs. It notes that Middlebury College found that the average GPA for students who took a gap year was consistently higher than that of those who did not. Skidmore College is reported to have documented that gap-year freshmen generally earn GPA's several percentage points higher than their peers.

******

Many of us have heard stories of students who enter college trying out different courses and majors, like the "meanderers" mentioned earlier. Some students pursue an academic field without an idea of what the related professional world of the area entails. Others follow their parents' expectations of what they should grow up to be. In some families, academic studies are easy for one sibling and the other feels inadequate when they don't thrive in a classroom setting. It's not unusual to find men and women who decades later are still searching for a career that is a good match for their skills and abilities and will offer them fulfillment beyond a paycheck. (We explore more about this in the upcoming chapter on "Gappers in the Workplace.")

Gap Years and Educational Direction

The majority of gap students in our survey said that their experience either confirmed or set them on a different educational and career path. Sixty percent said it either "set me on my current career path/academic major" or "confirmed my choice of career/ academic major." Thirty-two percent said it had some impact, but not as much as other factors. Eight percent report that it had no impact on their academic direction.

It's intriguing to consider what could happen if one discovers an academic direction that leads to a career interest before or during college that is tied to something he or she likes or even is passionate about. Those who are so fortunate may never have to "work" a day in their lives.

Bathsheba Demuth

Bathsheba Demuth, the self-directed sled dog apprentice and Brown University graduate, is one of those whose gap experience had an impact on her education and career path. "I am planning on doing a Ph.D. in history or anthropology as a direct result of my gap years and the research I did in college about the village where I lived – and I plan on going back north, so my gap years have been very influential. I learned that I really enjoy living in different cultures, learning new languages, and studying their history. Without gap time I probably wouldn't have learned this until after college."

Jon Teel

Jon Teel believes his experiences also influenced his academic focus tied to self-awareness as a global citizen that emerged during this gap year. Since then, Jon's experiences have included serving as the volunteer coordinator for HelpArgentina, a U.S.-founded 501(c)3 nonprofit organization. Its mission is "to strengthen Argentine civil society through the mobilization of donors and volunteers and the promotion of best practices." It was during the gap year that seeds were planted for his dream of living and working abroad.

After being wait-listed by his top college choice, Jon studied at the Oxford Tutorial College and lived with a host family in England. He then traveled to Hawaii as a participant in San Francisco State's Wildlands Studies program. His gap year included a home stay in San Miguel de Allende, Mexico, where he studied Spanish. Jon's mastery of the language helped him place out of beginning level Spanish courses during his freshman year at Davidson College near Charlotte, North Carolina. Echoing the reflections of other gappers, he found that his experiences gave him a different perspective from his peers when he was on campus.

Though I am an outgoing person and have always been wise about life (that is my opinion), my gap year gave me the confidence and knowledge to make good decisions and effectively skip many experiences that I saw my fellow students experiencing. I was clear about my objectives and intentions for college, but flexible and just energetic about the opportunity to spend four years in college. For example, while my fellow classmates were partying or procrastinating or struggling with adapting to being away from home, I was getting to know some of my professors better, making friends with older classmates, doing community service, and having profound conversations about life, college, politics, or whatever with others. I just looked for different things than many of my classmates at that time and I think that my gap year did play a role in that perspective.

Jon's gap year continued to shape his college career as he studied international relations in Switzerland and worked with youth from the Middle East for two years after college. When we last connected with Jon, he was realizing his dream through his role at HelpArgentina, first conceived during his gap year, of living and working overseas. He was continuing his studies as well, pursuing a master's degree in international relations. He concludes that his heightened awareness of other cultures and ways of living was a result of his gap year experience.

Julie Siwicky

For Julie Siwicky, the time she spent abroad in India and New Zealand impacted her academic direction: "It instilled in me a passion for traveling and learning about cultures different from my own. I also formed relationships with amazing people, whom

I continue to keep in touch with regularly. Finally, it played a large part in my decision to concentrate in Development Studies at college. I plan to use this degree to deepen my connection with other parts of the world as a professional."

Owen Genzlinger

Owen Genzlinger is one who found out what he loves to do during his gap year and tied it to his academic direction. His inspiration for taking time off came after seeing the impact gap experiences had on his brother's career choice.

Owen's brother took a break and found his academic focus and career. "My brother did a few different programs, one of which was the New York Film Academy. He then went back to the University of Texas in Austin and entered into the Radio Television and Film program. He figured out through a gap year what he really wanted to do. At the end of high school I was in a similar position so I figured I'd give it a try. I'm very glad I took the chance."

Owen's gap year started with a two-week Sail Caribbean course where he helped navigate fifty-foot boats and earned a water SCUBA diver certification. "It was a lot of fun to do something I have always been interested in but never really thought I would be able to do in my life time." He then spent "eighty-eight days to be exact" on a NOLS (National Outdoor Leadership School) semester in Arizona, New Mexico, and Texas. "We started off on an extended backpack trek for three weeks, then went on a three-week caving expedition. We then went out to Texas where we canoed down the Rio River back to New Mexico for a three-week rock climbing session. We wrapped up the trip with a twelve-day independent backpack in Arizona." In January, Owen went to New Zealand for three-and-a half months where he interned with a company called

Spike Fin that creates web pages for New Zealand businesses. He says, "That wrapped up my gap year, but I don't feel like it has really ended. I've continued to build on the things I've seen and done in that short year and I never stop thinking about my experiences."

Like other gappers, Owen returned with a renewed interest in education.

> I was ready to go to school after my gap year. I realized that it is worth pursuing the things you truly love, even if it is difficult at first. But once you get going, you'll be glad you weathered the storm and stuck it out because after things start rolling, you realize that you are doing something you truly love, and you start working hard again. You have to work for the things you love, and to make your dreams a reality. I had a dream come true when I got my private pilot's license, and I never thought that would happen. I think that the gap year experience prepared me to work hard for what I want and for what I believe in.

Owen wrote from the Spartan College of Aeronautics and Technology in Oklahoma, where he was a flight student. "I knew that I wanted to fly but I don't think I would have been as successful as I have been without those experiences. The things I learned on that time off from school are things you can't teach in a classroom. You have to experience certain things in order to learn them. The gap year also tested my beliefs. I was able to solidify some beliefs and question some others. You have to be willing to stand up for what you believe in and to not worry about the people that try to shake those beliefs."

******

Is a gap year worth it? The students and parents we've surveyed and interviewed report that gap years can have a positive impact when it comes to developing an interest in learning and success in formal education. The survey and stories we've shared underscore that most students:

- return to college within six months after a gap year;
- graduate "on time" compared to the national average;
- take school and learning more seriously;
- see their grades improve or remain competitive;
- emerge as more passionate and active learners; and
- say gap years have an impact on their academic choice and majors.

We've had the opportunity to talk with parents and students about these provisional findings. The reaction of a father who attended a Gap Year Opportunity Fair in Washington, D.C. is familiar.

"Would it make a difference for a young person to be able to connect with a passion before or during college in a way that made sense to them internally? In a way that made education 'real' for them? And in a way that set them on a life and career path that would allow them to continue to grow personally and professionally doing what they like or even love? That's a gift I wish I had received. That's a gift I want for my child," said a father. Many parents we talk to agreed with his sentiment.

******

Another parent, listening in, had a question. "That sounds great, but how much does it cost? With the cost of college already so high, is a gap year worth it?"

"Great question," we were able to respond. Our survey asked about the return on investment in a gap year – a question that prompted the observations in the next chapter on "Gap Year Dollars and Sense."

******

Gap Year Survey Findings Summary

- *Do gap year alums go back to college?* From our survey, 90 percent of students returned to college within a year and 80 percent within six months. Five percent returned within two years (a number of these students chose to take two gap years). Two percent were back in college within three years and 3 percent took longer than three years or did not return to college.

- *Do students apply to college before a gap year?* Seventy-seven percent in our survey applied to college before a gap year; 23 percent did not. Of those who applied, 93 percent were accepted to at least one college; 7 percent were not accepted to any college.

- *Do students apply for and receive deferrals?* More than half (56 percent) of those in our survey requested and received a deferral of admission.

- *How long does it take gap alums to graduate from college?* In the survey, 82 percent reported that they graduated in four years or less, after we factored out those still in school. Fourteen percent graduated in five years and 4 percent graduated in six years.

- *Do students take academic work more seriously after a gap year?* Sixty-six percent report taking academic work more seriously and 24 percent answered they regard studies "about the same" as before a gap year.

Eight percent said their attitude was somewhat less serious after a gap year and 2 percent report taking studies much less seriously.

- *What about grade point averages for gap alums?* Seventy-five percent of those answering the survey report earning a 3.1 or higher grade point average (34 percent earning 3.6 to 4.0 and 40 percent earning between 3.1 and 3.5). Nine percent went to colleges that don't use grades to measure academic achievement and 2 percent earned between 2.0 and 2.5 GPA.

- *Do gap years have an impact on academic direction?* Sixty percent of survey respondents said it either "set me on my current career path/academic major" or "confirmed my choice of career/academic major." Thirty-two percent said it had some impact, but not as much as other factors. Eight percent said it had no impact on academic direction.

Tips

- *Gap year friendly colleges.* A growing number of colleges are supporting – even advocating – gap years. Check websites and talk to admissions staff if you are curious about their view.

- *Gap year improving chances of college acceptance.* Improving your chances of getting into a particular college should not be a primary goal of a gap year. However, it makes sense that a gap year can help an applicant stand out to admissions staff.

- *Deferrals.* Consider applying to college and requesting a deferral. The vast majority of colleges *will* grant a deferral. They likely will ask for a brief description of what you are planning to do during a gap year so they can have assurance you won't just be hanging out at home on the couch. Plan on sending deferral requests and descriptions in the spring or at least before the first tuition payments are due. Let's Get Global was founded by Rita Golden Gelman whom you may know as author of *Tales of a Female Nomad: Living at Large in the World*, and more than seventy children's books. The organization is a great resource for those interested in gap years. It is compiling a list of colleges that grant deferrals. Here's the link: http://www.letsgetglobal.org/educators/colleges-granting-deferrals/

- *Applications.* The end game of a gap year is going to college. So if you don't have a deferral from the college of your choice, build the college application process into the gap year plan.

- *Changing college choices.* Gappers may change their mind about the best college for them during a gap year. This can be a good thing as his or her growing self-awareness is leading to more deliberate choices. If you defer college and change where you choose to go, you may lose the deposit.

- *Scholarships from colleges and universities.* Colleges and universities may not defer scholarships so you may need to reapply. Many schools say they try to hold scholarships for when the gapper attends college.

- *Federal aid.* If a student qualifies for federal financial aid but has deferred college, you will re-apply by completing the Free Application for Federal Student Aid (FAFSA).

- *Age and maturity on returning to school.* A frequently asked question is whether being older than their peers will have a negative impact on a gapper's college experience. We have not heard from any gapper that this was an issue. We have heard that gappers are more *mature* than their college peers. It may be worthwhile to seek out international dorms or similar living arrangements or organizations similarly-minded students are likely to join (e.g., cultural groups, etc.).

Chapter Four

GAP YEAR DOLLARS AND SENSE

"My year was one-fourth the price of a year in college and three times the education in life."

– Alison Moynihan

Not long into most conversations about gap years, the money question emerges. *How much does one of these gap experiences cost?* The question may be asked by a parent or student who's already stressed by the prospect of paying for college. It's easy to anticipate the parent's brain churning, calculating what it could mean to add even *more* cost to their child's higher education bill. The money question also is more prominent in recent years as an increasing number of students are delaying attendance in order to save for college.

The simple answer to the money question is: it depends. Parents and students can invest thousands of dollars in a gap experience, or they can participate in programs, internships, or jobs that help pay for college. In some cases, programs provide room and board in exchange for a gapper's labor, and offer scholarships and college credit to help defray costs.

te finances can act as a prompt for taking a gap
erviews, some students commented that a major
taking time off was that they "could not afford to
attend college," their "family didn't have money for my schooling
beyond financial packages," and they "needed to earn money to
pay for the rest of college." We've spoken with parents and students
who believed that the only option after high school if college
wasn't in the picture was to work at a grocery store or fast food
establishment. They have been surprised and relieved to find that
there are opportunities to earn money as a part of a plan that leads
to higher education.

Is It Worth It?

Perhaps there's another question parents and students should ask
in addition to the strict cost of a gap year: Is it worth investing time
and money in a gap experience? The answer to that question is not
as simple, so it is useful take a look at the factors that may add up
to dollars and sense for gappers and their families.

It's not surprising that many families are of two minds when it
comes to the value and the price of a college education. Eighty-
two percent of those responding to a Survey of Parents of College-
Bound Freshmen say "the cost is well worth it." The survey was
sponsored by Sallie Mae, an organization that offers students loans
and administers college savings plans. Parents and students believe
that the value of an investment in college today will be realized
in earnings and quality of life down the road, and there is data to
support this view. Looking just at the financial aspect, the College
Board, a not-for-profit organization known for the SAT assessment,

reports that the typical graduate of a four-year college will earn sixty percent more than a worker with a high school diploma over their years employed. Those with advanced degrees tend to earn two to three time as much as those with a high school diploma or GED. In addition, college graduates are more likely to be in jobs that offer health care and retirement benefits.

As confident as families are about the value of college, when it comes to paying the bill, that's another story. One reason is the generally rising cost of higher education. The College Board also keeps track of the average total price for attending college. The cost for an in-state public school (2012-2013) without financial aid is $22, 261 – this includes tuition ($8,655), room and board, books and other expenses. A moderate cost for a private college is $43,289. Many families receive financial aid to help lower the cost but are still left with a gap to pay the full bill.

Parents' behavior when it comes to saving for college doesn't necessarily align with their expectations for their child's future. Although most parents say they value college as important for their child's future success, their financial behavior doesn't always support this belief. While the vast majority of parents in the Sallie Mae survey believe college is worth the cost, a much lower number have a realistic understanding of how to pay for college. In a State of College Savings Survey, 66 percent of respondents do not know how much they need to save for college. Forty percent are "not very confident" that they will reach their savings targets. More than 40 percent in the survey say they've saved nothing for college. However, the majority haven't altered expectations about their child's attendance. Three-fourths of those responding to the survey report that they will be highly disappointed if their child doesn't go to college. Another financial factor, student debt, is also rising, up more than 800 percent since 1965 in real dollars. The average debt of students who graduate from public 4-year colleges is almost $26,000 according to a report from the Institute for College Access & Success's Project on Student Debt.

The fact that students are taking longer to graduate from college – an average of six years according to the National Council of State Legislatures – is adding to rising college costs and student debt. The total investment in time and money causes most Americans to pause with total price tag for six years exceeding $100,000 for public schools and a lot more for private institutions. There is some good news in that many colleges have doubled their aid to students over the past decade. Even with a generous award of scholarships and grants, however, it's no wonder that a parent or student would feel vulnerable when it comes to financing higher education.

So back to the question of "is the gap year worth it"? Parents and students may have saved and planned for years to invest a certain amount of money in a college education. Others are planning to take out significant loan amounts to fund college. Are gap year advocates suggesting that families should now add more cost, possibly multiplied, if there are additional kids in the family and the gap idea catches on? And the investment isn't just in financial terms. There's a time investment that leads to another round of questions. What if this is just a waste of time for my child when he or she could or *should* be investing time in college? What is the "opportunity cost" of not being in school – such as the commonly-expressed concern of a gap year student getting "behind one's peers" – regardless of the out-of-pocket cost of gap years?

******

In exploring the answer to a valid money question – Is the gap investment worth it? – we asked students and parents whether cost was a factor in considering and planning a gap year. We also asked how much their experiences cost compared to equivalent time in college. We wanted to know who pays for the gap year and, in terms of impact, whether gappers gain a sense of financial awareness. The survey asked whether gap students graduate in more or less time than their peers (potentially saving or costing thousands of dollars). It also explored whether gap students believe they are positioned to gain more or less from the investment in education than other students.

Like most Americans, gap families look at the price tag carefully, whether they are considering the cost of college or that of taking a break from formal education. Sixty-five percent responded that cost was a factor in gap year planning. Just over 2 percent, however, singled it out as the "most important factor." Comparing the cost of the gap year to higher education, 70 percent said that the cost was less than an equivalent time period in college. About half said it was "significantly less expensive." Eighteen percent said the cost was "about the same" while 8 percent reported it was "somewhat more expensive" and 3 percent said it was "much more expensive."

When it comes to paying for a gap year, all of the students contributed in some fashion by working, saving, fundraising, applying for scholarships or actively looking for programs that would pay them. However, the majority of students (68 percent) also had support from their parents or guardian. Thirteen percent paid for the entire experience themselves through working, saving, or fundraising. Seventeen percent of the students in our sample said that programs paid for their gap experience.

City Year – "Give a year. Change the World."

One example of a program through which participants can earn money is City Year, founded in 1988 by Michael Brown and Alan Khazei who were roommates at Harvard Law School at the time. Its motto is, "Give a year. Change the world." and its goal is to "unite young people of all backgrounds for a year of full-time service, giving them skills and opportunities to change the world." It is part of a network of programs affiliated with AmeriCorps that provide opportunities to participate in community service activities. Longitudinal studies of AmeriCorps alumni show benefits in educational achievement and commitment to service. We will explore the AmeriCorps research in more depth in an upcoming chapter on "Gappers and Serving."

One of the options within AmeriCorps is dedicated to programs for young Americans. This track is where City Year fits within the AmeriCorps family. There are several rewards a member can receive in exchange for completing a year of service, based on information provided on the AmeriCorps and City Year websites. One benefit is a weekly stipend for living expenses while serving in City Year. The amount varies based on the location of service, but we've heard from a number of corps members that it's minimal. Living on an extreme budget and taking food stamps is not an unusual part of the experience. After completing a year of service, members receive an award of $5,500 (2013 award amount) to apply toward undergraduate or graduate education. The award can also be used to pay off student loans. City Year provides basic health care insurance, uniforms, and a cell phone with 300 minutes of usage per month.

Another financial advantage of City Year and other AmeriCorps programs is that a growing list of dozens of colleges and universities across the United States will match or augment the education award through scholarships, course credits, or waiving registration fees. Some of the colleges that fully or partially match the education award and/or offer college credit for eligible undergraduate or graduate students include:

> Central College (Pella, Iowa)
> Duke University (Durham, North Carolina)
> Evergreen State College (Olympia, Washington)
> Hampshire College (Amherst, Massachusetts)
> Northeastern University (Boston, Massachusetts)
> Ohio Valley University (Vienna, West Virginia)
> Prescott College (Prescott, Arizona)
> Princeton University (Princeton, New Jersey)
> Southeastern University (Washington, D.C.)
> Syracuse University (Syracuse, New York)
> Union College (Barbourville, Kentucky)
> University of Arkansas (Little Rock, Arkansas)
> University of Delaware (Newark, Delaware)

There are other gap programs represented in our survey that pay or provide room and board. Our son, Adam, found a paying job in outdoor education as part of his gap year through the Student Conservation Association. Ceci Hughes and David Lofgren also found paid positions at an outdoor school run by a non-profit and the Washington Conservation Corps.

that, "about 80% of our fellows get financial aid and a full third are on 100% scholarship."

A few years ago, an anonymous donor committed $1.5 million to The University of North Carolina at Chapel Hill to support the Global Gap Year Fellowships program. The Morehead-Cain Scholars Program offers a four-year undergraduate scholarship to Chapel Hill and includes support for a gap year experience. There also is a Michael Brownstein in '99 Memorial Gap Year Fellowship Program. It was established to honor Mr. Brownstein who was "a young man with a strong humanitarian spirit and sense of social justice whose life was tragically cut short in a June 2007 accident, but not before he lived his life to the fullest, passionately pursuing life-affirming experiences through extensive travel."

College Credit

Another financial factor to consider is that a number of gap programs have formalized arrangements with colleges that allow students to earn course credit. Every course offered by the National Outdoor Leadership School (NOLS), for example, is approved for credit and three-fourths of students use this option. Dynamy (which is explored more in-depth the next chapter on "Gappers in the Workplace") offers three college-level courses to those who sign up for the Internship Year College Credit Option and participants receive credits through collaboration with Clark University in Worcester, Massachusetts. Global Crossroads offers volunteer and travel programs in thirty-four countries in Asia, Africa, Europe, and Latin America. Participants can earn up to 3.3 semester credits, depending on the length of projects they are involved in. Some language immersion and more academic programs also can result in college credit.

If getting college credit is part of the plan, our students recommend first researching the program offers and university partners. Based on experience, one gapper advises that being proactive about the option of college credit is far more preferable than trying to arrange for credit after a gap year.

Fundraising

In our survey, every respondent contributed financially to their gap year in some way. This can include working and saving. It can also include fundraising. Many students have participated in raising money for projects in their community – and the same strategies can apply for a gap year. Letter writing campaigns and seeking support from local businesses or churches can be effective. Going to local media also can work. A key is to be creative! Two gappers in the UK set up a YouTube channel to fund their gap year. Another cut his hair in exchange for gap year funds. The website Kickstarter (www.kickstarter.com) offers a way to invite friends and strangers to fund creative projects. Many program and other gap year sites have great information on fundraising. The international student exchange program, AFS, has a website with ideas ranging from finding a sponsor to walking dogs to hosting a golf tournament. Check it out at: http://afsfundraising.wetpaint.com/page/Fundraising+Ideas

Tax Deductions

Here's another tip for those interested in minimizing gap year expenses. When Adam applied to gap programs, we noticed that most were non-profit. A logical question seemed to be whether some or all program fees were tax deductible. We found that in a number of cases, they are. Some programs note the tax deductible status on their websites. Global Routes' site, for example, states "project contributions are tax deductible."

Other programs don't advertise if tax deductions are an option. We had to ask a New Zealand-based program whether their fees were eligible for deductions under the U.S. tax code. After several persistent calls, we found that the answer was "yes." Some internationally-based programs anticipate these kinds of questions in their promotional material. The website of the Peace Villages Foundation (which is headquartered in Venezuela), for example, states that, "Costs are referred to as donations since they are generally one hundred percent tax-deductible."

If a Gap Year Costs Money, Who Pays?

The gap year survey asked who paid for the gap experiences. As noted earlier, the majority (68 percent) were supported by their parent or guardian. A program covered the cost for 17 percent of students (these are primarily our City Year alums), and 13 percent paid for it themselves. Through interviews it became clear, however, that even students who were supported by parents contributed in some way to cover any associated cost.

Regardless of the level of direct financial contribution on the part of students, most report that investing in the experience directly leads to a greater return.

Lea Broh

Lea Broh's financial sense did not start as a result of her gap year, according to her parents. She had always understood the importance of saving money for the important things in life. So it was no surprise when we learned that Lea provided most of the funding for her gap year, which was marked by a three-month home stay and immersion in Chilean language and culture. It was important to Lea that she was able "to do this on my own, with my parents' only providing support with 1.5 plane tickets."

What did emerge, however, in both Lea's and her parents' estimation, was her ability to budget and manage her finances. According to her dad, Tony, Lea showed tremendous maturity in managing her money throughout her year in Chile, Costa Rica, and Greece. In Lea's words, the impact of her gap year on her financial awareness was simple: "I found that I could handle myself and my life. It was not a shock to me as it was to my peers in college, to live on my own, knowing that I can navigate on my own."

In Lea's opinion – and that of Tony, her dad – the gap year was more than worth it. According to Tony, the gap year investment was "miniscule" compared to a year of college. Among the returns that Lea saw was her ability to win internships and fellowships because of her gap year. And it was not lost on her parents that Lea's increased readiness for, and success in, college would be measured by her ability to graduate in four years, which she did. The consensus of Lea and her family is that gap years are "absolutely" worth it in the lessons learned and skills that emerge as a result. Tony's words to concerned parents are typical of what we hear from so many – "Kids are more capable than we think, especially when required by necessity."

Amanda Shoaf

We met Amanda Shoaf at a gap year seminar sponsored by the Forsyth County public school system in North Carolina. Amanda says she had no idea what she wanted to do after graduating from high school. "I had no idea what the heck I wanted to do with my life." Her mom, Kathy, agrees that it would have been "a disaster" for her daughter to head straight to college. Amanda discovered Up with People, a program established in the 1960s that is founded on the idea that music is a universal language. Participants travel the world while performing in staged productions and participating in community service – a great match for Amanda's interests. She made a commitment to pay for the $14,500 costs herself, and she did.

Amanda passionately believes that paying for one's own gap experience is an integral part of getting the most out of it. It turned out to be the best experience of her life so far. Her mom's face beams with pride as she talks about the enthusiasm and maturity her daughter, who proceeded to Appalachian State University, developed. Like many programs, Up with People participants can earn college credit and apply for financial assistance.

Malaka Refai

Malaka Refai's gap year experiences included volunteering at a shelter for street kids in Egypt, serving as a summer bed and breakfast manager in southern Chile, and working on an organic farm in Ireland. "I funded the gap year myself and I believe it made my experience richer. I knew I worked hard to have this experience, so it made it all the more mine. This also contributed a lot to my spending habits. I knew my parents would have helped me out if I needed it, but I wanted to learn about budgeting." You'll learn more about Malaka's experiences in an upcoming chapter, "Gappers in the Mirror."

Parker Stevens

Other students were fortunate to have their parent's support for portions of their gap year experience, but still benefited from growing financially more aware. This was the case for Parker Stevens, who wrote to us while studying abroad in Dar es Salaam, Tanzania. "I'm attending the University of Dar es Salaam for the semester and hopefully doing some traveling over the summer (if I have any money left over!)." During his gap year, he says, "I quickly learned how to budget and be much more aware of my financial situation – which is good now that I'm in college and my expenses are no longer covered by my parents."

Parker's journey began when he learned a friend was considering a gap year. "I worked extremely hard in high school. I went to an academically rigorous boarding school, and I knew that if I went to college after graduation I would burn out pretty quickly. A friend was looking into gap year options, and I became interested. The more I looked into what was available, the more I realized that I wanted to take some time for myself before college." Parker's itinerary included time in South Africa, Costa Rica, New Zealand, Fiji, and Australia. His experiences led him to study environmental science, and he hopes to pursue a career in environmental advocacy, health, or conservation.

When it comes to financing a gap year, Parker is another alum who believes it's important for students to contribute. "It's a good experience to be directly involved with financing your trip. I think that putting in the extra effort to raise/save money will make the trip that much more rewarding, plus you tend to be more aware of your budget if you contribute to it." In response to a question about the return on investment of a gap year, Parker replied "I would definitely say the gap year is worth it. If you have the opportunity, take it. After college, people tend to get so wrapped up in the business world that most of them would not recognize an opportunity like that, so take advantage of it while you have the time." Parker says taking a gap year is the best decision he ever made. You'll learn more about Parker's journey in the chapter on "Global Citizenship."

Parker's belief that students should help pay the gap year bills is shared by others such as Owen Genzlinger, whose gap experiences confirmed his love of flying. When it comes to finances, he believes, "You will own your gap year if you pay for it. It's OK to ask for help, to ask for money. It's intimidating, but people love to help when they see you're doing something different and doing the things you love."

Financial Awareness

Another area we explored is whether gap experiences result in increased financial awareness. What is the general impression of today's youth when it comes to financial accountability? If you count primarily on the media, the impression is that "financially responsible teenagers" is an oxymoron.

The image comes to mind of a generation smacked in the face by what some call the "kiss of debt," owing thousands of dollars and not very optimistic about their future. An anonymous contributor to a blog on "college grads and debt" writes that, "I don't think [high school] graduates are motivated to become students any more. One important reason is this debt problem that has become overwhelming." A survey by the investment firm of Charles Schwab presents a slightly more optimistic, although not overwhelmingly encouraging, picture. In the survey, fewer than half of teens believe they know how to budget money (41 percent). Fewer (34 percent) say they know how to pay bills or how credit card interest works (26 percent).

We asked students in the gap year survey, as one indicator of financial awareness, if they were more or less likely to accept credit cards and other "free" offers than their peers. The majority (51 percent) said they were less likely. Another 21 percent said they were about the same as their peers in terms of accepting a credit card offer. When we share this particular finding with parents, we generally get a raised eyebrow, smile, and head nod. The reason is the perception that credit card debt among college students is a challenge that many parents have no control over once their son or daughter has left home.

According to one study:

- 70 percent of U.S. college students have credit cards;
- five of every six of the students don't know the interest rates associated with their cards; and
- 75 percent of them don't know what the charges are if they are late with a payment.

When the credit card offers arrive in the mail, it appears that many sign on without asking any questions or learning about the implications of interest rates on money they've essentially borrowed. Does anyone over a certain age – who went to college in the 1960s or 1970s – remember getting credit card offers? According to Dr. Robert D. Manning, author of *Credit Card Nation* and Professor at the Rochester Institute of Technology, even in the 1980s, parents were required to co-sign for a card and credit limits were relative modest at around $300 to $500.

In recent years, the average student has been approached with about five credit card offers each month that are accompanied by "signing bonuses" ranging from pizza, candy, and t-shirts to iPods, according to the Higher Education Debt Project affiliated with the U.S. Public Interest Research Group. Due to thinner credit histories, students can be charged higher interest rates and penalties for late payments than those charged to other segments of the population. Some colleges and universities try to regulate or ban active marketing by credit card companies on campus, but students can still be reached through mail, email, and in other college town venues.

Recognizing the active marketing to college students as a problem, Congress passed and President Obama in May 2009 signed the Credit Card Accountability, Responsibility, and Disclosure Act (the acronym stands for CARD). A main goal of the act is to help protect young adults, including college students, from being targeted unfairly by credit card companies.

In addition to the specific issue of accepting credit card offers, we asked gappers if they grew more or less financially aware through their experiences.

- The majority (66 percent) say that after a gap experience, they are "much more" or "somewhat more" financially aware than their peers.
- Twenty-six percent say they are "about the same" as their peers in financial awareness.
- Four percent report they are "somewhat less" aware, and 1 percent is "much less" aware.

The awareness can develop through a combination of having to fundraise, live on a lean budget, and learn about the value of money through getting to know those who may be less fortunate than many Americans, at least in financial terms.

Sarah Pulitzer

Sarah Pulitzer is one alum who says she grew significantly in financial responsibility through her gap year. Sarah grew up in a small town – Durham, New Hampshire – and took the opportunity to go on a service trip to Costa Rica between her junior and senior years in high school. "I didn't know where I wanted to go to college, but after Costa Rica I wanted to travel and stretch my legs." Financial accountability was part of her plan from the beginning. "I worked all through high school to save up for spending money while traveling. I learned to budget."

During her gap year, she first went to New Zealand and took art classes for two months. The experience "solidified the idea that I could pursue art in education and even as a career." She then traveled to Fiji with the Institute for Cultural Ecology, lived in villages with thirteen other U.S. students for two months, and then interned at a resort where she surveyed coral reefs. The journey continued in Australia, where she served with Involvement Volunteers for one month.

In India with LEAPNOW for three months, she spent time with two leaders and five other gappers. "We went all over. We volunteered at an orphanage in Rishikesh that was run by an American woman. There was a little house in the Himalayan mountains where she took the kids when it got hot. She grew all the food for the kids – mostly Nepali whose parents couldn't afford to take care of them – so we helped plant the gardens. Then we went trekking in the Himalayan Mountains for ten days, close to Nepal. And then we traveled to an Ashran and visited a Tibetan Center." Sarah visited the UK for ten days and then returned home.

When we talked with Sarah, she had one semester left before graduating from Sarah Lawrence College in Westchester County, New York. She says "the real world experiences impacted my choice of academic concentration. And I can apply education to the real world."

Sarah offers several financial tips for those planning a gap year. If you're traveling abroad, look into a World Ticket that can save significant money. Look into an inexpensive cell phone and put a SIM card in it. "Other countries have different systems than the United States." Take one credit card and travelers' checks ("there aren't ATMs on every corner in India!"). And check into the exchange rate and travel insurance. (The American Gap Association – www.americangap.org – website has a good section on "Gap Year Financial Aid" that you may want to check out.)

When it comes to finances, Sarah recognizes that she is more fortunate than most. "Many of those at Sarah Lawrence have money (me, too). But the big difference is they haven't worked or budgeted. I have."

******

A number of gappers say their ideas about money changed through their exposure to poverty in different cultures, including in the United States. Eighty-three percent reported that a primary result of their gap year was that it "gave me a better understanding of other countries, people, cultures, and ways of living." One aspect of this impact was a heightened awareness of poverty and comparative wealth in the world.

Shoshanna (Shanna) Silverberg

Shoshanna (Shanna) Silverberg's experiences in Ghana, featured earlier in the "Journeys In Time" chapter, provided an understanding of poverty. She concluded from looking at the suffering associated with having low or no income that the "American dream doesn't connect with the world we live in." She resolved that, upon her return to West Hartford, Connecticut, and to college, she would live more simply and be less dependent on material comfort. This is a sentiment we found a number of gap alums acted on as they minimized their possessions upon returning home. As a result of her experience, Shanna says that she only recently "has become friends with money again." Mary Silverberg, Shanna's mom, notes that as a result of her gap year, Shanna has a "much clearer understanding of financial sacrifices," is more organized in dealing with money, and is conscientious in meeting her college loan obligations.

Alison Moynihan

Alison Moynihan's gap experience took her to Alaska where she learned carpentry and stone masonry, and to Bolivia where she lived with a host family and worked in a daycare center for children who live with their parents in prison. She then completed a twenty-eight-day survival course at the Boulder Outdoor Survival School in Colorado. Through her gap experiences, says Alison, "I became much more aware of my relative wealth and appreciative of the fact that my parents are putting me through college."

******

Some students change their minds about the college they want to attend or become more confident they are attending the school they chose before a gap year because of grounded reasons. "For some students, self awareness leads to a better fit," says Megan Kelly, who attended Oxford Tutorial College and traveled to New Zealand during her gap year. "The return on investment is that instead of spending money on a college that may not be a correct fit, a student will be able to make better decisions about which college to attend for their chosen field." As Megan points out, along with a number of other gappers and parents, it's also important to consider the cost of the "wrong college" or the price of touring through a series of majors.

Gappers also can be more conscious about the value of education and determined to get all they can out of it. In many cases, they already are comfortable navigating in the world outside of college with confidence. They may be more likely to look forward to integrating the world outside of academia into their future, rather than clinging to what some of their less-focused peers may perceive as the safe haven behind ivy-covered walls.

Dr. Jeffrey J. Arnett, professor with the Department of Psychology at Clark University and editor of *The Journal of Adolescent Research*, conducts research that is most closely associated with the concept of emerging adulthood. As noted in the earlier chapter on education, he makes the case that students should "meander" through college, trying out different subjects and strategies to discover what makes sense for them. We have heard from other educators that the purpose of fresh-man year is to foster non-linear exploration. They believe this explo-ration provides a solid academic foundation and leads to selecting or designing a major that is engaging and a good match. Dr. Arnett also suggests there is value associated with extra-academic experiences in young adult development, as when he writes in *Emerging Adulthood: The Winding Road from the Late Teens through the Twenties*:

> ...[E]merging adulthood is the time for trying out unusual educational and work possibilities. Programs such as AmeriCorps and the Peace Corps find most of their volunteers among emerging adults, because emerging adults have both the freedom to pull up stakes quickly in order to go somewhere new and the inclination to do something unusual. Other emerging adults travel on their own to a different part of the country or the world to work or study for a while. This, too, can be part of their identity exploration, part of expanding the range of their personal experiences prior to making the enduring choices of adulthood.

For some gappers, getting part of their education in the global classroom and spending less time in college while becoming more financially skilled – even budgeting – can add up to significant savings in terms of dollars.

Costs and Benefits

Based on the research and surveys, we can paint a picture of students' growth during their gap experience that can add up to a significant profit. Let's consider both sides of the ledger.

- On the cost side, programs can range in price and this factor can be a consideration for those weighing gap options. On the benefit side, there are programs that can pay you, colleges might grant credit for gap experiences, and there may be scholarships available to help cover the price.

- On the cost side, most students invest the time and finances to pay for at least some part of gapping. On the benefit side, helping pay for a gap experience helps a student "own" the time off and value the price of an education.

- On the cost side, taking a gap experience may mean that students can be older than some of their peers when they enter or return to college. A benefit, however, is that gap students tend to graduate in fewer years than the national average, saving tuition dollars. And most students say being a year or two older doesn't make much of a difference or that the added maturity can be a benefit in applying yourself academically and navigating the challenges that inevitably come your way.

Another big benefit is that many students appear to grow more financially aware. During a gap experience, most students had to budget and were exposed to other societies, cultures, families, and individuals (including in the United States) where individuals may not enjoy the relative wealth of many Americans.

Financial Advice from Gappers

We asked students and parents, "What would you say to a parent or student who is wondering whether a gap year is 'worth it' in terms of any money spent? Is there a value returned for the investment?" Here are the perspectives we have heard from those we interviewed.

Malaka Refai, whose gap year included time in Egypt and who funded her gap year herself, says, "I do not believe in putting a worth on experience. Experiences are the root of all lessons and a gap year is spilling with experience. I would recommend a gap year for anyone. I am a fuller person because of my gap year and there is no price tag on that."

Matt Byrne traveled to New Zealand for a gap experience that established his career direction as an aspiring reporter. He says that, "as long as a program is structured and legitimate, if you have to beg, borrow, or steal – do it!" He contributed between $4,000 and $5,000 out of his own savings and believes the investment is "part of the experience."

Leigh James, whose gap year included studying photography and ceramics in Mexico, reports that "the way I sold it to my parents was that they would spend more money on my fifth year of college that I would have had to complete if I didn't take a year off than if I took the year off. I definitely see the value returned in the investment because I am a stronger, happier person because I took time to figure out who I am. There was no way I could have had the same amount of personal growth in a year of college."

Erin O'Neil who spent time in Australia says, "I firmly believe that you cannot put a price tag on a gap year. You can always find the time or money for a college education, and most people get the same thing from a college education. What is far rarer is the opportunity to do something different where you can combine travel, education, culture, self-discovery, and adventure. I learned far more about myself and the world during the gap year than I did in four years of college. If I had gone straight to college, I think I would have felt lost. I would have felt like it was something I had to do, not something that I had chosen to do. After spending a year traveling and seeing things I had only dreamed of, I actually went to college wanting to be there."

We asked Wes Cannon, who "floored" his family after his gap experience with high grades and being a campus leader, about the return on investment of a gap experience. "There's an immense value returned. If a cost-benefit-analysis could be done, it would be very, very surprising. The experience you gain and the maturity and understanding of the world and your personal likes and dislikes could save you in many areas, such as: changing majors in college, the type of college selected; ease of finding jobs both in college and after; and the level of pay to someone with a gap year could be higher in my opinion than a normal college grad."

Alison Moynihan summarizes that "My year was one-fourth the price of a year in college and three times the education in life."

Parents' Perspective

Having been one of those sets of parents who made an investment in a gap year experience, we can testify to having assessed the potential costs and benefits closely. Adam decided to take a gap year fairly late in the game. It was in the spring of his senior year but before college deposits were due, so we had to have a clear idea of the financial obligation ahead. It didn't take much research to calculate the comparison between college (tuition and room and board at the colleges to which he had been accepted) and a gap year (program fees, travel overseas, and health insurance). The gap year was easily less financially exacting.

We also began to learn of ways to reduce these costs. This included cost-effective short-term health insurance, memberships in organizations that offered travel discounts, and tax deductions available through program contributions. Regarding health insurance, legislation enacted beginning in 2010 is designed to help young people stay on their parents' health insurance plan through the age of twenty-five even if they are not living in the family household or in school.

Adam's financial awareness grew exponentially through the year, as he began to appreciate the impact of exchange rates on his program fees in New Zealand, for instance. He also learned the advantages of living simply and "low impact" traveling. He subsequently planned a second gap year, finding a paid position as a counselor in a nature education center.

As a result of his second year and through his extensive gapper network, Adam found the perfect educational fit for him: Evergreen State College in Olympia, Washington where he could focus on his interests in the environment and science. Since his freshman year, he discovered the advantage (in tuition dollars) of being a state resident. He worked as a caretaker at IslandWood, an outdoor education center in Washington, to establish state residency and be eligible for in-state tuition. Along the way he met and married a beautiful and spirited Canadian, Allison, who has had her own gap-like adventures. They both earned scholarships and grants to pay for most of their education and graduated with no debt and even some money in the bank.

As an anecdote about linkages between gapping and careers (an area that we'll explore in depth in the next chapter), their first jobs out of college were leading students on international gap year programs for Carpe Diem. Carpe Diem "runs international academic programs that work with youth in an educational capacity to get them both out of the country and out of their comfort zones." The programs combine volunteering, cultural experiences, travel, language studies, and homestays.

More recently, Adam and Allison have launched the Pioneer Project, a gap year program in the Appalachian Mountains of North Carolina. Its mission is "to foster clarity of purpose, empowerment, and interdependence in young adults by offering a community-oriented educational experience focused on practical homesteading, craft, and wilderness expedition skills."

******

There is no guarantee that any aspiring gapper, or his or her family, will emerge as those we have surveyed and interviewed to see the financial benefits profiled here. We hope, however, that our findings can provide encouragement to those who take the long view about the pursuit of higher learning, as it is traditionally cast. The gap kids we have spoken to seem not to be in a rush to get back to college life, but they are ready. Once on campus, they report being fully invested and engaged in an enterprise they and their parents value so highly.

******

Gap Year Survey Findings Summary

- *Does a gap experience impact students' financial awareness?* In the survey, 66 percent said they were "much more" or "somewhat more" financially aware than their peers after a gap experience; 26 percent said they are "about the same" as their peers; 4 percent report they are "somewhat less" aware, and 1 percent is "much less" aware.

- *Is cost a factor in planning a gap year?* Sixty-five percent of survey respondents said it was a factor. Just over 2 percent singled it out as the "most important factor."

- *How much does a gap year cost?* In our survey, 70 percent said that the cost was less than an equivalent time in college. About half said it was "significantly less expensive." Eighteen percent said it was "about the same" and 8 percent said it was "much more expensive."

- *Who pays?* All students contributed to the gap year in some way – working, saving, applying for scholarships, fundraising, or looking for programs that will pay them. The majority (68 percent) had support from their parents or guardian. Seventeen percent said programs (such as City Year) paid for their experiences and 13 percent paid for it themselves.

Tips

- *Talk about money and budgets.* Parents/guardians and gap candidates should talk about the financial cost of a gap year early and often. Consider communicating about the gap experience in the context of a larger budget for college. This can be a "teachable moment" about budgeting and financial responsibility.

- *Paying for a gap year.* Students should have some responsibility for paying for a gap year. They can look into programs that pay you or offer room and board. They can contribute through working and saving during high school or as part of a gap year. They can research discounts on airfare and other costs. They can fundraise or apply for scholarships. Families also can plan part or all of a gap year with low- or no-cost options – working on a family farm, hiking in a park, interning, etc.

- *Research.* As we've mentioned before, researching gap year options – with or without a consultant – is essential and should include looking at the cost. There is not necessarily a correlation between price and the value an individual may gain.

- *Gap year scholarships.* Some programs offer scholarships or fellowships. If you are interested, check the website or contact the staff. It's a good practice to apply early. There are a few colleges (e.g., University of North Carolina, Chapel Hill) that offer gap year scholarships.

- *College credit.* Some gap year programs are affiliated with a college or university that can offer college credit for a gap experience. You might be able to arrange for credit with other institutions (a college that deferred you) so, if you are interested, ask – and ask early on in the process.
- *Tax deductions.* Some program fees may be tax-deductible. Check the websites and/or with an accountant or tax preparer.
- *Resources.* Here are three good resources for information and ideas on paying for gap years. Check out program sites for additional tips.
  - AFS (http://afsfundraising.wetpaint.com/page/Fundraising+Ideas)
  - American Gap Association (www.americangap.org/financial-aid.php)
  - Paying for a Gap Year Blog (http://www.thinkingbeyondborders.org/blog/blog/2012/08/02/paying-for-a-gap-year/)

Chapter Five

GAPPERS IN THE WORKPLACE

"I firmly believe that my experiences during my gap year set me apart from other peers in competing for a job. I believe my experiences show that I am confident, self-sufficient, a go-getter, someone who thinks outside of the box, and someone who has experience dealing with others who may be vastly different from myself."

– Erin O'Neil

Help wanted: Employees with good decision-making and problem solving ability, a commitment to teamwork, a strong work ethic, cross-cultural awareness, confidence in their abilities, and a great attitude.

A challenge facing employers in the United States and in many other countries is that there is a large and growing mismatch between the skills and abilities they need and those available in the current workforce. Numerous studies document that many employers have trouble finding qualified candidates. More than one-half are finding a poor match between employees' skills and those they need to run productive companies. The pending "retirement tsunami" of baby boomers is predicted to widen the skills gap, particularly for jobs that employers believe may require advanced knowledge. One may surmise that college graduates today who can demonstrate skills valued by employers will have a leg up on the competition, including global competition. (There's more about what the desired skills are coming up.)

How does a young person today develop the skills employers seek and might even be willing to pay more for? One theory is that experiences outside of the traditional classroom can help develop those abilities. To test the hypothesis as it applies to gap years, we looked for evidence from other countries on the connection between gap experiences and sought-after skills.

******

A specific focus of the U.S.-based gap year research is the impact that experiences may have on gappers at work. We wondered whether such a focus through the lens of American gappers would parallel the findings of research in the United Kingdom.

Researchers in the United Kingdom, where the modern gap concept originated, have investigated the relationship among gap experiences, careers, and employment. We set out to explore possible correlations between the skills developed by gappers in the UK and the United States, and if these were the same ones sought after by employers. The question we asked is: *Do gap years contribute to an emerging adult's preparation for success in the workplace?*

In this chapter, we explore several areas to help answer the question. First, we consider what the UK research says about gap experiences and work-related skills. Then we look at whether gap alums from the United States believe they developed skills and abilities through their experiences that are valued by employers. The next area is whether the abilities gappers report that they developed contribute to their success after their gap year and in the workplace. We also explore whether gap alums have found that their experiences interest employers and provide a competitive advantage when it comes to being accepted for a job. Finally, we asked about whether alums are satisfied in their careers at a time when other surveys show that most employees are not happy at work.

Research on Gap Years and Employability from the UK

As noted previously, the gap year concept in the United Kingdom has a comparatively long history; consequently, it has been the subject of both privately- and government-funded research. Three studies, in particular, address the intersection of gap years and work. These include:

- "Review of Gap Year Provision" research conducted by Dr. Andrew Jones and sponsored by the Department of Education and Skills in the UK;
- "The Milkround Graduate Recruitment Survey"; and
- "The Student Intelligence Report" by Hobsons/ Trendence.

Review of Gap Year Provision Research

First, we'll consider the conclusions of the "Review of Gap Year Provision" research. In 2003, the British government's Department of Education and Skills commissioned Dr. Jones to provide a "baseline overview of the policy issues surrounding gap years in the UK," including implications for employability and work. Dr. Jones noted in the preamble to his report, "because of the lack of existing research and literature on the topic," it was important to conduct some original surveys, interviews with "gap year providing organisations" and a "small number of interviews with nine young people."

His report, "Review of Gap Year Provision," published in 2004, offers a comparative framework for American surveys and qualitative research. Jones found that there are an estimated 200,000 to 250,000 young people in the UK between the ages of sixteen and twenty-five who take gap years each year, and this number is increasing especially for "post-school" (before college/university). (By 2012, the number had jumped to 2.5 million, according to the *Student Times*, the UK's national student newspaper.)

Regarding the nature of gap experiences, Jones offers that gap years in the UK include a wide-range of activities, both structured and unstructured. He defines a gap year as "a period of three to twenty-four months which an individual takes 'out' of formal education, training, or the workplace." He also concluded that gap years are perceived to be beneficial experiences in which "participants gain a wide range of life skills and other more specialized skills, skills which employers often identify as ones lacking in new recruits."

The Milkround Graduate Recruitment Survey

Research from the Milkround Survey also concludes that gap years may add to employability. Milkround is a commercial "graduate recruitment firm" that has been in the forefront of UK-based research on the impact of gap years. (The UK term, "milkrounds," refers to employment interviews conducted by graduate recruiters.) A 2006 Milkround graduate recruitment gap year survey asked 378 respondents if they believed their experience had made them better candidates for employers. Of the 50 percent who had already taken a gap year, the overwhelming majority (88 percent) said "yes," their gap year had "added to their employability."

These UK gappers identified personal skills development as the principal outcome of this employability focus. Specific attributes gap year alumni developed include adaptability, self-reliance, the ability to self-motivate, independence, flexibility, adventurousness, and understanding others.

The Milkround survey also asked those who were planning to take a gap year what they saw as the potential benefit of their experience. In response, one-third pointed to career-oriented benefits, specifically "gaining transferable skills" or "having some extra time to decide what to do for a career." The particular skills that those planning to take a gap year were hoping to develop included:

- learning a new language;
- gaining professional skills relevant to their career;
- acquiring training in practical skills; or
- working toward a teaching qualification.

These findings from the Milkround survey also help lay the groundwork for points of comparison with American gappers, especially in terms of perceived benefits from taking gap years in the area of employability or career focus. A complementary report from the student research firm of Hobsons/Trendence provides additional clues and points of comparison that help answer the questions about gap years and employability.

The Student Intelligence Report

Hobsons/Trendence is a private survey research firm and "the largest provider of student research across the UK and Europe." Its primary customers are employers who want to uncover the latest trends in graduates' opinions on careers, employers, and recruitment. Hobsons/Trendence developed "The Student Intelligence Report, 2006" (SIR) to discern the ethnic composition of the graduate market. It also added "a very scientific approach to monitoring the future aptitude and skill sets of the population, via a partnership with the market-leading psychometric assessment company SHL." The SIR survey included 25,699 university students as participants, about 10 percent of the total graduate population, according to SHL, the principal partner in the survey. According to the authors of the report, it was "the largest survey of graduate opinion on careers, recruitment, and employers in the UK." This large representative sample (1) included students who had gap year experiences; and (2) provided data that linked specific "skill sets" or competencies with those activities typical of a gap year.

The basic characteristics of the survey sample – what the report calls "Student Profiles" as identified by the Hobsons/Trendence Planning and Research Division – include the following:

- 10 percent were eighteen years of age or below;
- 37 percent were nineteen to twenty years of age;
- 31 percent were twenty-one to twenty-two years old;
- 10 percent were twenty-three to twenty-four; and
- 12 percent were older than twenty-four years of age.

These ages correspond to those identified by the Jones report as typical of gap year students. In regards to level of education:

- 84 percent of students in the survey were undergraduates;
- 9 percent were postgraduates; and
- 4 percent were in professional or doctorate level studies.

The Hobsons/Trendence Student Intelligence Report (SIR) survey correlates gap year experiences with more articulated competencies or skill sets (the same ones that we included in our survey and follow-up interviews and that are referred to as the Great Eight competencies). Competencies are defined as the knowledge, skills, and abilities earned through formal or non-formal education, work experience, or in other ways that will lead to successful performance in a job.

SHL (the principal partner in the SIR survey) is a well-known provider of employee selection assessments in the UK, Europe, and internationally. For the survey, SHL occupational psychologists distilled the skill sets or competencies most important for positive performance in the workplace from a larger competency framework. The Great Eight competencies are defined in terms of behavioral outcomes by SHL experts. In both the survey and follow-up interviews, we referred to these same outcomes when asking gap alums to identify the skills and behaviors they developed as a result of their experiences outside the traditional classroom. The definitions of the Great Eight competencies are provided below.

- *Adapting/Coping.* Developed confidence in my ability to handle situations of uncertainty or ambiguity where definite information or direction was unavailable. Was able to bounce back quickly from setbacks and difficulties that arose and maintain an optimistic outlook. Developed an ability to adjust my interpersonal style to other people's characteristics or to situations, including using humor.

- *Analyzing/Interpreting.* Learned how to speak and/or write in a way that captured people's interest and that others found engaging. Found that I could ask questions and probe for information when necessary to solve problems where there were vague or confusing issues. When faced with the need to solve a problem, I found that I could produce a range of solutions and identify the most workable solution.

- *Creating/Conceptualizing.* Was able to learn new techniques or master new information quickly. Questioned traditional assumptions and became more open to new ideas. Tended to see alternative ways of approaching problems and identified new ideas that others had missed.

- *Enterprizing/Performing.* Became more confident in my abilities and the likely success of projects or tasks that I undertook. Was able to tackle demanding tasks/projects and work through challenges to achieve success. Found ways to achieve goals while avoiding unnecessary waste and using resources economically.

- *Interacting/Presenting.* Found that I could speak and act in such a way as to persuade people to undertake a task or work harder on a project. Established rapport with others. Developed strong working relationships that enabled me to accomplish tasks and achieve goals. Found that I could manage disagreements and resolve conflict between myself and others.

- *Leading/Deciding.* Learned how to work well on my own and handle problems without having to seek guidance from others. Found that I could take calculated risks when I had adequate information and had analyzed a situation.

- *Organizing/Executing.* Easily accepted direction from others and was receptive to being managed. Improved my ability to identify priorities and take steps toward achieving objectives. Found that I could manage time effectively by allocating realistic timetables to get things done.

- *Supporting/Cooperating.* Found that I could relate well to those of different backgrounds, including those from diverse ethnic, religious, or cultural backgrounds. Learned how to communicate feelings and thoughts rather than suppressing them. Developed a better sense of who I was as a person.

At our request (and as facilitated by SHL colleagues in the UK), the Hobsons/Trendence team conducted secondary analysis to help correlate, if possible, the Student Intelligence Report findings with our own. The first challenge was to ensure that we could compare our sample, particularly in terms of age, with the SIR sample. With an average age of 21.6 years, the UK sample matched up well with that of the U.S. gap year participants in our survey.

Secondly, we needed to identify the categories of participants in the SIR study whose extra-academic or gap activities fit most closely with the U.S. students. The UK researchers, of course, were very familiar with the gap year concept and concurred with our hypothesis that two categories – those who had traveled extensively or had been involved in volunteer/charity work – would be most closely aligned with American gap experiences for the purposes of the research comparison. Based on this alignment, here is how the UK gappers ranked responses to the question, "Which three of these skills are you best at?"

1. Organizing/Executive (49 percent)
2. Supporting/Cooperating (48 percent)
3. Leading/Deciding (42 percent)
4. Adapting/Coping (41 percent)
5. Analyzing/Interpreting (40 percent)
6. Interacting/Presenting (31 percent)
7. Creating/Conceptualizing (25 percent)
8. Enterprizing/Performing (15 percent)

U.S. – UK Gapper Competency Comparison

The next step in answering the question about whether U.S. gap year experiences can lead to skills valued on the job was to ask the question: *Do U.S. gappers develop skills similar to those developed by UK gappers that are valued by employers?* If this proved to be the case, a hypothesis may be that gap year experiences are valuable to employability and career-focus among similarly-situated young adults. And that this is a common thread across gappers in at least two countries, the U.S. and the UK.

In developing the U.S. survey, we used the Great Eight competencies described earlier as a basis of comparison between the UK and American gappers in order to get more detailed responses on the development of skills. The relevant question in the survey asked gap alums to rate the competencies that they believe they developed as a result of their gap year, similar to the question asked in the UK research.

The results show a strong correlation between the U.S. and UK results. Both groups ranked Adapting/Coping, Leading/Deciding, and Supporting/Cooperating in their top four out of the eight competencies. Employer surveys and our experience as workforce development consultants support the finding that these also are skills that employers value. The exception was that the UK groups ranked Organizing/Executing in the top spot, where as the U.S. gappers ranked it sixth.

These findings support the more global findings of the UK Milkround survey and Dr. Jones's report on the importance of skills such as these for employability. The size of the Hobsons/Trendence sample and the use of the Great Eight competency model lends credibility to the results of the much smaller Milkround survey, for instance, that gappers point to the importance of their experiences in developing skills such as "adaptability" and "flexibility" (Adapting/ Coping), "self-reliance" (Leading/Deciding), and "understanding of others" (Supporting/Cooperating).

******

Many of the American gappers cited employment-oriented reasons for taking gap years, as did their counterparts in the UK. Recalling that one-third of the Milkround respondents pointed to career-oriented benefits, specifically "gaining transferable skills" or "having some extra time to decide what to do for a career," the U.S. sample of 273 gappers identified similar motivations for their gap years. In response to the question, *What were the most important factors that entered into your initial decision to take a gap year?*, a significant percentage chose employment-related factors. For example, 46 percent wanted "to take time to explore possible career paths or courses of academic study (majors)" and 29 percent wanted "to gain additional experience or education/training in an area of specialty" as motivation for pursuing a gap year option.

For U.S. respondents, participating in internships held a prominent place among gap experiences and would be logical choices for those, in particular, who cited career-oriented factors as big contributors to their decision. Seventeen percent of our respondents indicated that they chose internships or worked in the U.S. and an additional 24 percent reported that they did internships or worked abroad.

Partially as a result of these findings, and of the specific inclusion of gappers from the U.S.-based Dynamy internship program in our survey, we anticipated a significant number of respondents would have a career-orientation. What we did not anticipate is that gap years would have such an impact on changes in career direction or choice of academic major. As mentioned earlier, about one-third of U.S. respondents attributed the career direction or choice of major to their gap year where their experience led them to change their minds as to career choice. Another quarter responded that their gap year experience confirmed their career choice or major. These findings attest to the fact that internships or work experiences in general can help young adults discover what they want to pursue as a career.

Perhaps as important, they may discover what they do *not* want to pursue. We've heard from several gappers, for example, who thought they were headed toward a medical profession. (In more than one case this projection was due to expectations and hopes of a parent.) After test-driving the field of medicine during a gap year, their choice of academic major shifted to passions closer to their hearts.

Dynamy

Fred Kaelin is Executive Director of Dynamy, a program that includes a focus on internship and career exploration. Dynamy, headquartered in Worcester, Massachusetts, offers gap year programs that integrate living in a city apartment, internships, career/college guidance, and wilderness leadership opportunities. Fred is a knowledgeable supporter of the hypothesis that gap years can have a strong positive impact on employability and career direction. Dynamy's forty-plus years of experience in the field has taken these factors into account by requiring students who stay with the program for a year to participate in three different internship experiences.

In an interview, Fred recounted examples of interns over the past ten years who were convinced that they were in the perfect place in terms of a career focus during their first internship experience. After a second and third work-based experience, they thanked Dynamy staff for encouraging them to consider additional options. Many more examples of the Dynamy graduates point to the pivotal role of internship experiences in helping young adults "discover their passion" while making valuable contributions to one of the programs' 250 business sponsors.

The Dynamy internship experience as a gap year option is a more intense experience than comparable school-based programs. In the Dynamy design, interns are expected to work thirty-five hours a week for nine weeks. With a typical internship class of thirty-to-forty per year, Dynamy's program oversight includes visits with the employer sponsors and ongoing evaluation of the interns' experience. One conclusion that has emerged from this extensive and intensive experience with employers is that young people without college degrees can do a lot more than they think they can. Interns have the opportunity to contribute in real terms and are held accountable for the quality of their work because their efforts may be key to business success.

Andrea Chace Wessling

Andrea Chace Wessling is an example of a Dynamy intern whose experience helped point her in the direction of a college major and potential career. After seeing a connection between school and the world of work, Andrea's internships helped her narrow down a choice of academic options. "I think it made me much more focused in my pursuit of education. I knew I was going to college, as far as I and my family was concerned, that wasn't really a question. But for what? To do what? After becoming trained as a sexual assault hotline counselor during the course of one of my internships, and after taking an offered course on gender, race, and class, I decided that I would focus on women's studies. I also think the experience made me appreciate my intellectual capabilities more."

Andrea also noted that her gap experiences helped her earn employment after college. "My experience working with Worcester Rape Crisis and then training to become a rape crisis hotline counselor impacted my understanding of a lot of issues pertaining to the field of women's studies. ... Training as a sexual assault hotline counselor helped me get the job as a domestic violence counselor after college."

Kate Wheatcroft

Kate Wheatcroft is a Dynamy alum who is cofounder of Bien Cuit, a bakery with several locations in New York City, and a growing wholesale operation related to bread and pastry. Kate was noted as one of Forbes's "30 under 30." Here's what Kate says about how Dynamy helped her focus on a career in the food industry.

During my time at Dynamy I found out not only what I
wanted to do, but how much I could do. The program gave
me the supported freedom to explore my interests and
realize the extent of my strengths. I worked on a farm and
in political organizing and found myself drawn to particular
elements of both jobs that would later feed my career in
the food industry. As an organizer, I learned what brings
people together and motivates them and how to turn those
big ideas into practical solutions. On the farm, I learned the
first step in making a meal: the harvest or the slaughter.
My respect for food and the importance of where it comes
from is directly linked to those months I spent at The Heifer
Project chasing pigs out of the vegetable garden, gutting
turkeys, and learning to plant tomatoes.

Gap Years and Employability

We were curious about whether there were other alums, like
Andrea and Kate, who believed their experiences contributed to
landing a job. In our survey, respondents were asked to rate on
a scale of one to ten the relative benefits of their gap year. One
such benefit was the extent to which their gap year experience
"impressed employers and helped me get a job or better jobs than
I might have without it." Of those responding to this question, 46
percent rated their gap years as having strongly contributed to
improving their employability (ranking this response as an eight,
nine, or ten on a scale of one to ten).

In follow-up interviews, we asked gappers if they found employers
to be interested in their gap experiences and if they had found their
experiences "an advantage to your getting a job or other success in

the workplace." Erin O'Neil, whose experiences included time on several continents, responded:

> I firmly believe that my experiences during my gap year set me apart from other peers in competing for a job. I believe my experiences show that I am confident, self-sufficient, a go-getter, someone who thinks outside of the box, and someone who has experience dealing with others who may be vastly different from myself. These experiences helped me obtain a summer internship at a local non-profit. My employer was surprised and thrilled to hear about the volunteer work I did, especially involving land and animal conservation, as her non-profit dealt with similar issues.

Katherine Evans

We met Katherine Evans at a conference on gap years that took place in Raleigh, North Carolina. Katherine took a gap year in between sophomore and junior years at the University of North Carolina at Chapel Hill. Her gap story started with a sophomore slump and ended with a distinctly career-oriented focus. She wanted assurance that the academic direction in communications she was following was building toward something concrete in the real world.

She decided to take a dip in a journalistic pool to figure out if there was a connection between what she was studying in the classroom and what she thought she would need to apply on the job as a reporter. She took what she describes as "an internship gauntlet" with a series of four journalism-oriented internships near school including working in public radio, as a reporter, and as a free-lance writer. Her discoveries led to her successfully connecting the academic-work world dots. As one indicator of the impact of Katherine's experiences on career choice, she wrote "The Gap Generation," an article that appeared in a 2009 edition of *Carolina Alumni Review.*

Seth Owen

Seth Owen's gap year experience opened his eyes to new experiences and helped instill an entrepreneurial bent that influenced his career choices. He became the "man of the house" at the age of fifteen when his father passed away. His resulting depression made it difficult for him to make the most of his experience at Middlebury College in Vermont. His mother and grandparents encouraged him to consider a gap year.

His plan for the year included an internship at the Sheridan School in Luray, Virginia, for the fall. The Sheridan School is located in the Shenandoah National Park on a 130-acre campus. The curriculum emphasizes "adventure, teambuilding, and hands-on social studies programming." For the second half of the year, he worked in Costa Rica as a teaching intern with kindergarten students. He counts among his successes his work with one student, Kevin, who had limited social skills when they met. Seth worked one-on-one with Kevin three days a week and was gratified to see that Kevin could be integrated in regular school activities after four months of their being together.

Seth credits this experience for nurturing his entrepreneurial spirit and his developing fluency in Spanish. When he returned to pursue his education and transferred to the University of Vermont, he began to realize the contribution of the gap year to his sense of financial responsibility and appreciation for education as something he was doing for himself. He was more personally motivated about his education, not going through the motions to meet the expectations of others. He was excited to return to school with a broader world view and a zest for learning.

As a real estate developer in Colorado – and a veteran of two small company start-ups –the self-motivated young professional has learned to deal with objections by not taking things at face value. What is Seth's principal piece of advice for a prospective gapper ("not a coaster") who is interested actively in their own development? "Immerse yourself in some dreams."

Broadening Skills Employers Value

Another way of framing the advantages that gappers have found when interviewing with prospective employers is that their experience enables them to speak concretely about skills and abilities that they have demonstrated in unique and sometimes trying circumstances. They are able to distinguish themselves from others without just depending on GPA, college reputation, or courses of study.

In the words of Hannah Kane, a City Year volunteer in Boston and Washington, D.C., gappers can articulate the distinction between just "talking about things" and "doing things." A common part of a job application process can be a behavioral interview. In this type of interview, candidates are asked for specific examples of how they have used abilities which are needed for success in the position they are applying for. Gappers can be specific in linking experiences with skills or behaviors they have learned such as those found in the Great Eight competency framework.

An interviewer might ask for an example of working and communicating in a cross-cultural team for a position with an international firm. The gapper might be able to talk about experiences living with a host family in another state or country and working through seeming communications and cultural barriers to build a relationship. The question might be about being proactive in learning new skills and professional development in a company in which the market environment is constantly changing. The candidate might give examples of having to learn new skills "on the fly" and developing options for how to help his team solve a problem, build something, or grow something.

This ability to frame one's experience into a coherent narrative is an outcome of gappers' getting to know themselves better. It almost goes without saying that the decision to take a gap year in and of itself can attest to self-directedness and being open to new experiences.

Becca Krass

Debbie Krass, mother of Becca whose gap year led her to be a motivated student at Williams College, attributes her daughter's interest in moving to Los Angeles "cold" with no leads to a career in the entertainment industry to an intrepid nature – and skills acquired as a result of her gap year experiences. Debbie recalls that it took guts for her daughter to venture to a new city. "She went to LA to pursue her dream of being a producer in the entertainment industry. She was scared. She didn't have any contacts. But she went! She confronted her apprehensions. She found work, went to work, began in the mailroom, and became an assistant. She got a chance to look around and realized female agents don't have lives and children, and that life style wouldn't work for her. It took guts for her to go there. And it took guts for her to decide, 'this isn't for me.'"

******

We've heard from a number of gappers that they are more open to a wide variety of career options and diverse job opportunities as a result of non-traditional experiences. We frequently talk with college seniors who are not gap alums and who are facing a challenging job market. We also sense there may be a somewhat different attitude and approach among gap alums in the same situation. It's understandably frustrating to try to find a first job when a lot of employers aren't hiring or would prefer someone with experience. A number of well-intentioned seniors have told us their main challenge is that their college isn't helping them connect with job opportunities, they don't have access to the right network, or even that their parents (who they look to for leads) are in different careers from where they want to make their professional mark. Some regret not looking for internships and other work experiences during college, many of which are no longer open to them once they've graduated, because they didn't know about them or it didn't occur to them.

A number of the gap students we've seen in similar situations learned how to establish and grow broader networks during their gap experiences. Their résumés may stand out from the crowd, but they also have more developed competencies in areas such as:

- Leading/Deciding (handling problems without having to seek guidance from others and taking calculated risks with adequate information);

- Adapting/Coping (confidence in the ability to handle situations of uncertainty or ambiguity, able to bounce back quickly and maintain an optimistic outlook, and adjust interpersonal style to other people's characteristics or to situations); and

- Analyzing/Interpreting (communicating in a way that others found engaging and when faced with the need to solve a problem, finding a range of solutions and identifying the most workable solution).

These areas serve them well when faced with a challenging job market.

Gappers also believe their experiences helped them expand upon their repertoire of skills and broaden their knowledge, often in ways that would not be possible in a typical college curriculum. Around 85 percent of U.S. survey respondents rated their gap years highly (eight to ten on a scale of one to ten) when it came to providing them with "additional skills and knowledge that contributed to my career or academic major." The survey also asked gappers to assess their growth in skills and knowledge pre- and post-gap year – and how they viewed their skills in comparison to their peers. Forty percent of students said they believed their skills were higher than their peers before the gap year. The number rose to 73 percent who believed they had higher skills than their peers after a gap year.

Viewed together with the finding on the gap year's influence on college major or career choice, this positive comparison suggests that alums consider their gap year beneficial to their growth in skills relative to their peers.

Matt Byrne

In interviews with gappers we asked, "Have your gap experiences influenced your ideas of what you want to do for a career?" Matt Byrne applied to, and received a deferral from Goucher College in Baltimore, Maryland, prior to his gap year. As a result of his three-month experience as a reporter for a New Zealand newspaper, he decided to go into a career in journalism and chose Emerson College in Boston because of this interest. His gap year had a career focus and puts him among those in our survey who reported that they "wanted to take time to explore possible career paths or courses of academic study (majors)" as one of the prime reasons for taking a gap year.

During his time in New Zealand, the regular reporters went on strike and Matt carried out significant tasks for the paper, rather than acting as a "go-for" or as an "article clipper/fact checker." Reflecting on the career-oriented skills and knowledge that he gained during his time in New Zealand, Matt said that his experience taught him that, in reporting, "everything you need, you have to go out and get. You have to become more a student of other people." He also said that he had to impress upon his interviewees that he was genuinely interested in their stories.

He added that he had to be creative, especially because he had to write under tight deadlines with the added pressure of knowing that his articles were going to be published and others would read them. He learned to master short-hand, interviewing techniques, and the specifics of layout, all the while negotiating with the reporters on strike as a condition of performing his duties as a reporter.

Expanded Networks

In the context of workplace success, we thought that as a result of their experiences gappers would come to understand the importance of networking and develop broader connections than they had previous to their gap year experiences. Reams of research and the direct experience of almost everyone who has worked substantiate the value of networks for knowledge and information sharing, collaboration, solving problems, and job satisfaction. As noted earlier, networking can also be of assistance when seeking employment opportunities. The ubiquity of Facebook, YouTube, or LinkedIn illustrates the power of social networking on a person-to-person basis through the Internet.

With this background in mind, the survey asked how frequently alums were still in contact with those they met during their gap year. Almost 40 percent reported being in touch at least once per month with gap year acquaintances and almost 30 percent said they were in touch at least once in the last six months.

In addition to frequency of contact, we were interested in the impact of the gap year on broadening a gapper's relationship circles. The survey asked: *"After your gap year, compared to before your gap year, how broad a circle or network of friends or acquaintances did you have?"* More than 70 percent reported having a broader set of connections – one-third said that their social network was "much broader" after their gap year, and 40 percent said that their network was "somewhat more broad."

There also is the potential that the diversity within these networks is greater post-gap year as well as being broader. Considering the experiences of those who served abroad and City Year volunteers who serve within diverse work groups, gappers are more likely to define a "much broader" network in terms that include the nature and not just the size of those groups.

For Hannah Kane, who worked for a non-profit organization, Action Without Borders, her City Year experience was pivotal to her appreciation of networking: "It's difficult for me to remember what my career plans were before joining AmeriCorps. I think I wanted to be a filmmaker. That changed. I don't know if it's directly because of my gap year experience or not, though. I can certainly trace all of the jobs I've had since to a City Year contact. It did good things for my social and professional networks."

Job Satisfaction

The survey asked employed gappers about their level of job satisfaction, sources of job satisfaction, and also to consider how they might differ from their peers (primarily students) who are not part of the workforce. Among this group we also interviewed a number of alums who had taken their gap years ten or more years ago. Their stories illustrate the impact of their gap experiences on their work lives over time.

Roberto Latino

Roberto Latino's experiences in Istanbul, Turkey, provided him with the opportunity to travel extensively on his bicycle and discover the wonders of the ancient world. From the perspective of the workplace, however, the lessons he learned from his discoveries are still relevant today. Roberto looks back on his experience in Turkey in the mid-1990s as a highlight of his life. Among the many insights he gained was that "ancient times are not all that ancient... the ancient world is still alive." As a result of his explorations of archaeological sites in Turkey, especially seven early Christian churches, Roberto developed a "sense of line" in architecture.

Most importantly from a career perspective, he gained an appreciation for the beauty and utility of tile work in central Cappadocia. In his business, he seeks to replicate the ancient Turkish tile art in building and repairing homes. His subsequent employment included a tour in the military, where he learned valuable skills as a mechanic and a continuing appreciation (developed during his time in Turkey) for the ability "to do a lot with a dollar."

Kathy Olson

Kathy Olson has had the benefit of several decades to reflect on her gap experience and see its impact on her career of social service and non-profit management. She currently works for the United Way leading a number of community-strengthening projects which help adults to improve their workplace skills. Kathy's self-initiated gap year after graduating from a mid-west high school in the mid-1970s consisted of travel to Italy where a member of her family was serving in the armed forces. From this "home base" her study of European art led her to traverse the length and breadth of the Italian peninsula until it was so familiar that Italian travel became "second nature."

The time she took in Italy to serve as a volunteer tutor for young children who were having problems in school had a longer-term impact. This experience led her to major in speech pathology and audiology with a minor in art when she returned home and attended the University of Iowa. Her interest in education extends to this day, where she still finds time to serve in schools while leading volunteer committees and community-based groups in improving educational opportunities.

Jon Teel

Similar to Kathy Olson, Jon Teel has a perspective from his gap year that continued to inform his work for a non-profit organization in South America, HelpArgentina. Jon observes:

> While my gap year was a long time ago now, it continues to play a role in my life. I see it as the foundation for the various jobs, studies, and experiences that I have had ever since. So yes, many skills and abilities that I have now are a product of

this process that started back in 1998 with my gap year. I am also more satisfied with the decisions that I have made with respect to work...I am now living and working in Argentina with a non-profit organization to strengthen other non-profits through volunteer work, fundraising, and institutional support. Again, much of this is a product of what began with my year off.

******

Veteran gap alumni who have had the benefit of workplace experience and perspective can look at the depths of their careers in terms of job satisfaction, and especially the sources of job satisfaction. In responding to our survey:

- 53 percent of the employed cohort reporting that they are "very satisfied" in their career/job;
- 14 percent say they are "satisfied";
- 18 percent say they are "somewhat satisfied";
- 7 percent are "somewhat dissatisfied"; and
- none reported that they were "very dissatisfied."

Our survey findings contrast with a report from The Conference Board on job satisfaction in the United States that includes a focus on less-seasoned workers. The survey concludes that "Americans are growing increasingly unhappy with their jobs." In looking at younger workers, the report shows that, "Newer entrants are least satisfied. About 50 percent of workers under the age of twenty-five are satisfied with their employment situation."

With more than 76 percent of employed gap year participants – such as Roberto, Kathy, and Jon – reporting that they were either "very satisfied," "somewhat satisfied," or "satisfied" with their jobs these findings suggests that gap year experiences may be contributors to a young person's success in the workplace or career.

The survey also asked about sources of job or career satisfaction among respondents. When given the opportunity to select from a variety of sources of job satisfaction, gappers chose personal growth and development (71 percent) and the ability to help others (67 percent) over the status of a job (22 percent) or financial security (21 percent) that their jobs provided.

******

The power of the many examples from the interviews and the perspective provided by the gap year survey results suggest that something different may be going into the work ethic of gap year alums. Though gappers acknowledge the contribution that their experiences have had to career choice, employability, development of skills and social networks, what they have gained from their gap years is not measured by a sense of economic utility. Rather, they seem to think about work differently, more in terms of a fulfillment of a passion they discovered in working with others (in the case of teachers), helping communities or families solve problems (as non-profit organization managers), or seeing themselves as empowered to start their own businesses. They find opportunities where they not only can make a difference, but also where they can become engaged.

Dr. Barbara Schneider, a labor economist at the University of Chicago who specializes in the transition of young adults into the workplace says such engagement can emerge when we encourage young people "to take part in activities that challenge their abilities and give them opportunities to increase their skills." In her book, *Becoming Adult*, she points to research of Dr. Mihaly

Csikszentmihalyi (pronounced cheek-sent-me-high-ee), professor of psychology at the Claremont Graduate University in California.

> Csikszentmihalyi refers to such balance as being in a flow state, when the adolescent is so absorbed in an activity that he or she loses track of time and feels at one with the activity. Spending time in flow promotes learning and the acquisition of skills. Persons who seek out challenges that are equal to their expanding abilities are more likely to develop a positive view of their lives. ... Such self-directed persons strive to achieve goals that are intrinsically motivating. Having such goals means that the activity itself brings enjoyment and satisfaction.

We believe, based on our research, that gap year experiences can provide this sense of engagement which gappers then seek to replicate in their subsequent academic, volunteer, and work experiences. Gap year experiences seem to provide challenges and opportunities that lead to skill development.

******

The differences between the U.S. and UK approaches to gap years might be related to the American focus on college access and college admissions as a "rite of passage," as opposed to part of a more long-term, skill development focus. The latter is embodied in the implications of UK graduate recruitment surveys, like that of the Hobsons/Trendence study, for the employer market. Stated more simply, the focus on being accepted to college in the U.S. may be seen as a marker of "success," whereas in the UK the *kinds of skills* young people take into the workplace from an employer's and policy perspective may be more telling.

It is not our intention to suggest that the positive workplace or career outcomes of gap year experiences are a recommendation for gap years to become a main stream practice. We do offer the observation that during their gap years, young people make discoveries that enable them to see the world of work as a venue for engagement – as opportunities to continue to expand their view of the world and contribute to the well-being of others. The result can be a benefit to the gapper, their teams, their customers, their organizations, and their communities.

******

Gap Year Survey Findings Summary

- *Do some students want to take a gap year for employment-related reasons?* Yes. In our survey, for example, 46 percent wanted "to take time to explore possible career paths or courses of academic study (majors)" and 29 percent wanted "to gain additional experience or education/training in an area of specialty."

- *Do students work or take internships as part of a gap year?* Of those answering the survey, 17 percent indicated that they chose internships or worked in the U.S. during their gap year; an additional 24 percent reported that they did internships or worked abroad.

- *Do gap years help individuals gain work-related skills?* About 85 percent of U.S. survey respondents rated their gap years highly (eight to ten on a scale of one to ten) in terms of providing them with "additional skills and knowledge that contributed to my career or academic major." Almost three-fourths (73 percent) believed they had higher skills than their peers after a gap year compared with 40 percent before a gap year.

- *Do gap years expand one's network of connections, friends, or acquaintances?* In the survey, 70 percent said they had a broader set of connections as a result of a gap year.

- *Are gap alums satisfied with their careers and/or jobs?* Eighty-five percent of those employed in the survey said that they are satisfied with their jobs (53 are "very satisfied," 14 percent are "satisfied," 18 percent are "somewhat satisfied"); 7 percent are "somewhat dissatisfied"; and none are "very dissatisfied."

- *What are their sources of job satisfaction?* The primary sources of job satisfaction are "personal growth and development" (71 percent) and the ability to help others (67 percent) over items such as job status (22 percent) or financial security (21 percent).

Tips

- *Work-related activities as a gap year option.* Including a work-related component in a gap year can help one change, confirm, or test out a career direction.

- *Competencies and skills employers value.* Programs, parents, and educators can help gap alums recognize that they have developed competencies and skills that are related to success in work as well as in school and life.

- *Resumés.* Gap alums should consider including their experiences on their resumés in terms of competencies (e.g., Leading and Deciding, Adapting and Coping, Analyzing and Interpreting) that employers will recognize and value.

- *Interviews.* Gap alums should be prepared to describe and discuss their experiences with prospective employers in terms of competencies backed by specific examples from their time off.

Chapter Six

VOLUNTEERING AND SERVICE

"The most important aspect of my gap experience was doing community service."

– Maggie Hurreau

This is the pledge that members, including gap year students, take when they join AmeriCorps:

I will get things done for America -
to make our people safer, smarter, and healthier.
I will bring Americans together to strengthen our communities.
Faced with apathy, I will take action.
Faced with conflict, I will seek common ground.
Faced with adversity, I will persevere.
I will carry this commitment with me this year and beyond.
I am an AmeriCorps member, and I will get things done.

Each member receives a pledge certificate with the expectation it represents a commitment to "get things done for America" during the service term as well as in the years ahead.

In our survey, 69 percent of respondents included service as part of their gap year – 27 percent volunteered in the U.S. and 42 percent went abroad. We asked our alums about their commitment to continue volunteering after taking a gap year. We also asked about the benefits of participating in service activities compared to studying, traveling, or working or interning in a more traditional capacity. We looked at whether gap alums see serving others as a source of career satisfaction compared to their peers. As in the area of the workplace, researchers in the United Kingdom have addressed the topic of volunteering that we are able to use as a basis for comparison with gap years as they are evolving in the United States.

It's not a departure for Americans to dedicate themselves to volunteering. It's an integral part of many lives in the United States. Alexis de Tocqueville observed more than 170 years ago that a commitment to service is a defining characteristic of American life. He saw that the "voluntary alliances" that brought people together for a common good differentiated the relatively fledging United States from its European roots. He wrote in *Democracy In America*: "Americans use associations to give fêtes, to found seminaries, to build inns, to raise churches, to distribute books, to send missionaries to the antipodes; in this manner they create hospitals, prisons, schools."

Today, de Tocqueville would find that volunteering is stronger than ever in the U.S., with teens – including many gap students – representing one of the more active service groups in our country's history.

******

The tradition of youth service in America accelerated in the early 1900s. In 1906, Harvard University professor, psychologist, and philosopher William James gave a speech on "The Moral Equivalent of War." The address painted a vision for young

Americans' volunteering to serve, focusing on what he believed would be positive outcomes for individuals and the larger society. He called for, "a conscription of the whole youthful population to work on many of the toughest jobs." Those who served "would have paid their blood-tax, done their own part in the immemorial human warfare against nature; they would tread the earth more proudly, the women would value them more highly, they would be better fathers and teachers of the following generation."

Many established volunteer organizations that are active today, including in the gap year arena, were founded in the decades that followed. Rotary was founded, for example, in 1910, and Kiwanis and Lions Clubs were founded in 1916.

In 1960, then-Senator John Kennedy challenged students at an address at the University of Michigan to serve the United States through promoting peace by working on projects in developing countries around the world. The Peace Corps was born in part from that vision. Since then, more than 210,000 volunteers have served as corps members in 139 countries.

The area of service among American youth has been a particular focus of national leaders in recent decades, and a topic of much research. The volunteering rate of teenagers (ages sixteen to nineteen) in 1974 was 20.9 percent, but it dipped to 13.4 percent by 1989. To help counter the downward trend, Congress passed and President George H.W. Bush signed into law the bipartisan National and Community Service Act of 1990 that established provisions to help promote "service-learning programs for school-aged youth." In 1993, President Bill Clinton signed the National and Community Service Trust Act to help promote volunteering by Americans, including teens. The legislation established AmeriCorps, among other provisions.

The national leadership combined with grass-roots mobilization efforts had an impact. The Corporation for National and Community Service says that the rate of teen volunteering is on the rise. A report documents that 15.5 million teenagers volunteer annually, contributing more than 1.3 billion hours of service. That's a rate of 55 percent, more than double the rate of volunteering adults.

Internationally, volunteerism has also been on the rise in recent years. The 1980s saw an increase in organized volunteering in Great Britain, Canada, Australia, Holland, France, and Japan, among other countries. The United Nations announced 2001 as the International Year of the Volunteer, calling on almost one thousand international partners to participate, and including a focus on service among international youth.

AmeriCorps Survey

One of the goals of the Corporation for National and Community Service in the United States is to "measure and continually improve our programs' benefits" through research. In 2008, the Corporation released the results of a longitudinal study of the impact of serving on AmeriCorps members in areas such as careers, volunteering, and life satisfaction. The study was conducted with the research firm Abt Associates. It tracked 2,000 AmeriCorps members for eight years after service, and contrasted findings with a comparison group. The study found that AmeriCorps alums are more likely than the comparison group to enter careers in public or not-for-profit service with 60 percent choosing to work in these fields. It also found that members report they are more attached to their communities and more likely to participate in community events than the comparison group. About 80 percent of members report that they were exposed to new career opportunities during service and more than two-thirds report that their service was an advantage in the job market. AmeriCorps members report they are more satisfied with their lives eight years after serving compared with those who did not serve.

The Corporation also released a study that found that volunteering has positive impacts for teens, including those from less advantaged backgrounds. The study is based on feedback from 3,178 young Americans between the ages of twelve and eighteen. The report shows that benefits from volunteering, contrasted with a comparison group include:

- 70 percent believe they can make some difference or a great deal of difference in their community, compared to 51 percent in the comparison group;
- 66 percent say they are very likely to graduate from college, compared with 51 percent in the comparison group; and
- 52 percent say they are likely to volunteer within the next year, compared with 15 percent in the comparison group.

The Corporation's then-CEO, David Eisner, commented that, "This study highlights service as one of our most effective and positive interventions in a young person's life. For youth at risk of hopelessness and despair, service builds social networks, trust, confidence, skills, initiative, and lots of other tools that can help them succeed in life."

Gap Year Survey

Our survey asked similar questions of gap alums, including those who participated in City Year, which is affiliated with AmeriCorps. Our survey asked participants to indicate the impact that gap years had on them from a list of seven options. The options are that the gap experiences:

- impressed employers and helped in getting a job;
- provided additional skills and knowledge that contributed to my career or academic major;
- led to a better understanding of other countries, people, cultures, and ways of living;
- led to a better sense of who I was as a person and what was important to me;
- enabled me to build a broader network of acquaintances;
- provided a better understanding of international affairs, how America is perceived by others; and
- offered the opportunity to serve others or make a contribution to a cause.

We divided the participants into two groups – the first was those who participated in volunteering or service during their gap years (volunteers) and the second was non-volunteers. Of particular interest is how the two groups saw "the opportunity to serve others or make a contribution to a cause" as being a positive result of a gap year.

Both volunteers and non-volunteers had the same top two answers for the most significant impact of gap experiences. Both groups reported that the top answer is that the gap year "gave me a better sense of who I am as a person and what is important to me." The second answer for both groups – volunteers and non-volunteers – is that the gap year "gave me a better understanding of other countries, people, cultures, and ways of living."

However, there is a significant difference in how the two groups ranked "provided me with the opportunity to serve others or make a contribution to a cause." Volunteers ranked it *third* in the list of options, while non-volunteers ranked it *second-to-last.*

This finding appears to align with the AmeriCorps data that indicates those involved in volunteering activities see that they can make a difference in the lives of others. It also aligns with the AmeriCorps finding of a link between participating in volunteering during a gap year and the appreciation of the "opportunity to serve others" as a positive result.

In looking at the longer-term impact, however, serving others emerges as a high priority for gap alums who were employed at the time of the survey. The finding was presented earlier in the "Gappers in the Workplace" chapter that employed gap alums report a high level of job satisfaction with 67 percent "very satisfied" or "satisfied" in their job and another 18 percent reporting they are "somewhat satisfied." This compares with about 50 percent of their peers in a Conference Board survey who report being happy in their current jobs.

Our survey asked participants to rate seven sources of job satisfaction on a scale of one to ten. The seven options they were asked to rate were:

- status;
- financial security;

- helping others and being in involved in solving problems;
- the potential that I have to grow and develop new skills;
- work/life balance;
- the ability to travel; and
- "I don't look to my career/job as the principal source of satisfaction."

Again, we divided participants into two groups – volunteers and non-volunteers – to determine if there are similarities or differences in what they reported. We also excluded college students from both groups, as the question of sources of career satisfaction generally is not applicable to undergraduates who are not in the workplace. In particular, we were interested in how volunteers vs. non-volunteers ranked "the satisfaction that I derive from helping others, and being involved in solving problems" as a positive aspect of their job or career.

The result is that both groups ranked helping others in the top two answers, with "the potential that I have as a person and develop new skills" rounding out the top two for both groups.

Volunteers, however, rated "the satisfaction I derive from helping others" as significantly higher than the non-volunteer group. The volunteers, on a scale of one to ten, gave helping others a 6.3 compared to 4.71 among non-volunteers.

One provisional conclusion for why the volunteer group gave "helping others" a higher rating is that serving has an impact that persists over time and may be integrated into a work or career ethic. Even though the opportunity to serve others was second-to-last among seven responses for non-volunteers after a gap experience, it emerged as number two out of seven options of sources of satisfaction in careers or jobs. Both groups rank serving others higher than participants in other surveys on sources of job satisfaction for millennials, or the generation born in the year 1980 or after.

Versant Solutions – a U.S. marketing communications firm – conducted a survey of 100 college students and recent graduates in the U.S. and Canada. For the report, "Millennials: Engaging the Next Generation of Talent," participants were asked "what is the most important thing you want out of a job?" and given ten options. The options in order they were ranked were:

1. enjoyment/satisfaction
2. compensation
3. experience
4. good coworkers/atmosphere
5. security/stability
6. challenge
7. flexibility
8. *giving back*
9. communication
10. location

Thirty-three percent of participants in the Versant Solutions survey identified "enjoyment/satisfaction" as the most important thing in a job and 18 percent ranked money or compensation as most important. Three percent ranked giving back as the most important aspect of their work.

Robert Half International, a firm specializing in recruiting for the financial industry, and Yahoo! HotJobs, surveyed more than

1,000 millennials. The survey asked about top concerns for young adults regarding job opportunities. The number one answer was salary/healthcare/retirement benefits (33 percent) followed by job stability (26 percent) and career satisfaction (23 percent).

A survey of 1,000 young people led by FreshMinds Talent – a UK recruiting firm – concludes that millennials are "generally more ambitious, more brand conscious, and tend to move jobs more than ever before."

It may be tempting to generalize, based on surveys such as the three noted above, that millennials may be motivated by external value and brand status. Painting a generation with a single brush, however, doesn't do justice to the respect for individuality that is engrained in the American fabric. The individuals in our research illustrate that there are young Americans who, given the inclination and opportunity, find value in serving others, in part, as a way to discover themselves.

Eric Miller

Eric Miller is one of the students who received satisfaction from seeing the impact of his volunteering work during his gap year and his ability to make a difference. When we talked with Eric, he was enrolled in a Ph.D. program studying physics at the University of New Mexico. Eric was one of the students in the survey who took a gap year because he wanted a break from school. "As I was graduating from high school, I had been accepted into a few colleges, but had no real drive to attend. Boring classes had seriously stifled any desire I had to learn, so I took a year off."

Eric took a six-month break, spending time in Australia and England. "In Australia, I joined the Conservation Volunteers

Australia (CVA) program in Brisbane for six weeks, and volunteered at a local zoo in Cairns for six weeks. In England, I spent my whole time enrolled in the Totnes School for Guitar Making, during which time I built an acoustic bass guitar."

It was the volunteering experience that Eric recalls most favorably. "One of the more rewarding activities I participated in was the conservation work I did with CVA. CVA is a program that tries to improve the natural and wildlife areas of Australia, partly by removing invasive species imported from elsewhere around the globe. I greatly enjoyed this in part because of the satisfaction in looking back and seeing the significant effect that our work had achieved."

Another impact was a realization that he could step off the beaten path during his gap year journey and learn more about himself as a person and what was important to him. Eric says, "The change of pace during the year off really allowed me to realize that I can choose my own path, rather than just going to college because it was the next step. I ended up making that choice anyway, but it was a deliberate choice that I made, rather than following an agenda."

Another change during Eric's gap year was the time he devoted to reading, resulting in a change of career direction. "Leaving the monotony of high school and taking the year off refreshed my interest in education. I came back with a strong desire to attend college and learn things. Specifically, while abroad I had read Stephen Hawking's *A Brief History of Time*, and wanted to know much more about the subject. So, I took this interest and changed my major to physics."

Like other students, Eric has felt a long-term transformational affect from his time away and from volunteering. "The most significant impact the gap year has had on me is to change my outlook on life. In this way, it has affected everything I have done since in (from my perspective) positive ways."

Does Volunteering Continue?

As did the AmeriCorps longitudinal study, our survey looked at the impact that volunteering had on the likelihood that participation in service activities would continue after a gap year. In an AmeriCorps survey, 64 percent reported "volunteering in the past twelve months." Our gap year survey results also found a strong commitment to volunteering among alums. Of those who participated in the survey, 80 percent volunteered or were involved in charitable work in the last twelve months. Fifty percent are involved once a month or more frequently. One might conclude that the number of gap year participants surveyed engaged in service is comparable to or greater than the AmeriCorps sample.

Matt Hendren

Matt Hendren is a City Year alum who was featured in the "Journeys in Time" chapter and who continues to serve after his City Year experience. Matt Hendren was interested in a gap year after he realized he was not excited about the prospect of going to college.

Matt participated in two years of service through City Year in Boston. Catherine Hendren observes that her son gained clarity and maturity through the experience. She adds "that level of maturity and knowing yourself is hard to come by. I think it would be difficult to gain in a first year of college. In City Year, you have to make your own path, be responsible, and make decisions that impact others all the time. Your peers don't have the opportunity to develop that level of responsibility with a scheduled life sitting in lectures, playing sports, among other activities."

Catherine also notes the passion for service that Matt brought out of the City Year experience, and the respect he has for people from all walks of life. "There are almost two hundred kinds of different backgrounds brought together through City Year. Poor and wealthy, from all over the United States. They were brought together in teams of ten or twelve. Some didn't have GEDs yet. Others were ready for dental school. Talk about differences in gender and race, and the opportunity to develop cross-cultural understanding!"

When he arrived at University of North Carolina, Chapel Hill, as an "old" freshman, Matt was distinguished from his classmates by his lack of interest in purely social activities, wanting to cook for himself, and making outside reading a priority. He credits his time in Boston with his returning to school with enthusiasm, the ability to manage his time, and an interest in getting actively involved in campus life. He came to Chapel Hill with a commitment to offer to others what he had learned about the value of serving during his time with City Year. He created Carolina United, a program which is offered to student leaders before the fall semester. In his senior year he served on the Student Advisory Council to the Chancellor of the university.

A memorable City Year moment for Matt and his parents was Cyzgy, City Year's annual conference that brings participants together to hear speakers, participate in competition, and receive rewards. Cyzygy is derived from the Greek word "syzgy" that means "a rare alignment of celestial bodies."

"It was a wonderful, moving event," recalls Catherine Hendren. "We got to hear the national service story from all sides, and it gave us a more informed understanding of the movement of national service and what it could provide not just for Matt, but for all different kinds of people. It turned us into even greater converts."

Matt's advocacy for City Year's ethic of service continues to extend to others and has motivated many others included our son, Adam. Matt's enthusiasm for gap years demonstrates that sometimes giving back means giving others permission. Now Matt is one of the first to ask, "what are you going to do your service year?"

Volunteering and Careers

Our findings note that for 60 percent of respondents, the gap year experience had an impact on their academic major or career choice. An AmeriCorps survey found that service could be a pathway to careers in the public service or non-profit sectors. The interviews we conducted showed a similar, qualitative connection between volunteering during gap years and the choice of a career in the non-profit sector. Teresa Obrero, for example, is the City Year alum who was the first in her family to graduate from college and earned a master's degree in social work and non-profit management. Her goal is to help students from lower-income families gain access to higher education. Eris Dyson, also from City Year and a student at Notre Dame College in Ohio, is dedicated to a career that combines serving, poetry, and advocacy. When we spoke she was looking forward to attending graduate school in non-profit management. Kathy Olson traces the origins of her career with the United Way leading initiatives to help adult learners to her gap year in the mid-1970s in Italy where she served as a volunteer tutor.

Maggie Hureau

Maggie Hureau set out looking for an opportunity to volunteer and "somewhere along the way" found a career in serving others through City Year. Maggie decided to take a break because she "wasn't comfortable fulfilling the expectation to go to college directly after I graduated high school." Her brother had taken a gap year so her parents were supportive of her decision, but she received a different reaction from counselors at school. "Generally my school counselors assumed I had no interest in pursuing my education. Because I wasn't going to college I was not smart. Generally, I think people completely misunderstood my year of service." Looking back, she believes that "I needed to prove to myself that I didn't need a college degree to contribute to my community and be a strong leader."

After high school, she began a year of service with City Year based in Boston and working with a team of seven corps members in an after school program in Dorchester, Massachusetts. "The most important aspect of my gap experience was doing community service. All the work I did was in service to the community and the city as a whole. I had an enormous impact on the students I worked with everyday – middle schoolers, who were in my after-school program."

In serving, she learned more about herself and, like others in our research and the AmeriCorps survey, gained confidence. "There is a lot of value in the independence a person must have during a gap year. There is no doubt in my mind that it gives you a better perspective on what kind of person you want to be and what kind of career you want to pursue. It is an invaluable experience to give so much for one year – and shockingly, reveals more about yourself that you could ever imagine."

Maggie attributes her year of service with her career direction. "I loved my gap year so much I wanted to provide the opportunity for other people to have one. Now I supervise over twenty young people doing similar work to the work I did seven years ago. ... Doing my gap year helped me come back to the same organization [City Year]. Somewhere along the way I have decided to dedicate my career to the service field."

She also credits City Year with helping her develop skills that have helped her succeed in school and in work, such as time management and communication. "When I first started college I would complete my work two weeks before it was due. I also believed I gained some very important communication skills. While other students found it perfectly acceptable to pass in an assignment late without informing the professor, I would call, email, or talk to them before hand. I took greater responsibilities for my actions because in my gap year I learned the importance of my actions. I learned that I could do excellent things – and there is great responsibility in that belief."

******

The rise in recent years of U.S. student volunteerism is due, in part, to schools and youth organizations' encouraging service. There has been an increase in service-learning programs among high schools, and a number of colleges and universities have a community service requirement.

Schools in the United States tend to measure commitment to volunteerism by the number of hours dedicated to service and the corresponding dollar amounts. It's not unusual to see a press release from a college stating that the "campus community donated 40,000 hours with an economic impact of $640,000 during this past year." The Corporation for National and Community Service in 2006 initiated the President's Higher Education Community Service Honor Roll to recognize colleges and universities with strong commitments to serving. AmeriCorps studies show that students participate in volunteering most often when they are asked to, generally by a teacher in the context of service-learning.

The result for some students who are asked to participate in an isolated period of volunteering hours may be to look at service "in a box" or as what you do during a specific few hours at the request of a teacher or because of a school requirement. Based on interviews with gap year students, participation in service over a more extended period of time can result in a commitment and ethic that is more integrated into their lives. Courtney Camp's journey of service taught her how service to others and a compass can help find direction for life.

Courtney Camp

When we caught up with Courtney Camp, she was a third-year law student at the University of Washington in St. Louis, looking for a job with a public interest law firm in New York City. Her friends were asking why she wasn't going for the big bucks and a prestigious law firm, but she says her gap year spent serving others pointed her in a different direction.

Courtney is a sixth-generation Texan who left her home state and headed to a university in the East. Two years later, she found herself caught up in the partying scene and unsure about where she was going in school and in life. She met some students who had taken gap years and decided she would step off of the "on track" to think about her options.

She volunteered in Houston in the fall. Then she served in Kentucky teaching environmental education at the Pine Mountain Kentucky Settlement School, receiving a nominal salary and room and board. The school, founded in 1913, is located in the mountains of Appalachia in Southeastern Kentucky. It was the vision of William Creech, Sr., a local man who was focused on social challenges, health problems, and lack of educational opportunity in the region. Creech donated land to build the school that now covers 625 acres on Pine Mountain, hosts numerous plants and animals to support its focus on hands-on environmental education, and is a National Historic Landmark.

At Pine Mountain, Courtney learned she can "make something work for me," even in an environment very different than that she grew up in. She learned that "it is possible to confront fear when you're doing something meaningful." Specifically, she had to overcome her fear of snakes in order to teach a curriculum that included handling the reptiles. Also while in Kentucky, she became friends with local men who were coal miners and could have gone to college. Instead, they stayed near home, working in the mines to support their moms. Moving back to Texas was "something of a culture shock" because of the socioeconomic contrast, and she missed the outdoors.

She transferred to Rice University and found she was much more interested in education, "comfortable on her own," able to succeed "in any environment," and got better grades. We asked Courtney if there was a specific incident that she remembered from her year of service. She says, "I learned how to navigate with a compass, and teach others how to use a compass." She adds that the opportunity to serve others "changed my direction, and changed my life."

******

The observation that there is an inter-connection between giving to others and self-discovery is a frequent, and even passionate, observation shared by gappers as they reflect on their gap experiences. These reflections are included in next stage in the time off journey as we invite gappers to share the impact of being immersed in other countries and cultures at home and around the globe.

******

Gap Year Survey Findings Summary

- *Is the impact on gappers who volunteer different than on those who choose other experiences?* In the survey, volunteering gappers rated "provided me with the opportunity to serve others or make a contribution to a cause" third in a list of seven options related to the impact of gap years. Non-volunteers ranked the item second to last.

- *Do gappers who volunteer as part of their experiences transfer that interest into their careers?* The percentage of gappers in our survey who volunteer and report that their job satisfaction is derived from "helping others" is significantly higher than the non-volunteer group (although both groups ranked helping others high compared to their non-gap peers).

Tips

- *Build on previous volunteering experiences.* Most high school students have volunteered by the time they are considering a gap year. When weighing options, you may want to build on the interest in past service experiences.

- *Friendly to budgets.* In considering a gap year budget, volunteering is an example of an experience where programs may provide room and board in exchange for service or even a stipend or award that can be applied toward college or to pay off student loans (e.g., AmeriCorps programs).

- *Where to volunteer?* Gappers can volunteer or engage in service activities in the U.S. or overseas. There are advantages to each.

  Volunteering in the U.S. Although there are numerous diverse cultures in the U.S., there may be fewer practical barriers (e.g., currency, language, laws, etc.). You don't need a passport or visa. You might spend less than international experiences on, for example, airfare. It may be easier to stay in touch with friends and family.

  Volunteering Internationally. You may be challenged more out of your "comfort zone" than in the U.S. You can become immersed in a different language and culture. You may learn to travel more independently. You can more easily take a break from modern conveniences (e.g., TV).

Chapter Seven

GLOBAL CITIZENSHIP

AT HOME IN THE WORLD AND SEEING HOME THROUGH THE EYES OF OTHERS

*"I would say the most valuable part was the time when
I wasn't a tourist, where I was living in this culture,
living with this family who completely accepted me, and
completely took me under their roof."*

– Ben Ewing

In the United States today, many view global citizenship as a desirable goal, especially for youth. Abigail Falik is founder of Global Citizen Year, a program that brings high school graduates together through apprenticeships in the developing world. Her goal is to develop "a pipeline of new American leaders with an ethic of service, the fluencies needed to communicate across languages and cultures, and the ability to lead the next generation to address the challenges of the 21st century."

Abigail is among those who view global citizenship as an opportunity and a responsibility. Her early experiences abroad led to her interest in expanding opportunities for young people to immerse themselves in other cultures. As a girl, she traveled with her family throughout Asia, Africa, and Latin America.

> When I was sixteen, my sense of self and the world was
> blown open when I spent a summer in rural Nicaragua.
> Living with a family and teaching in the community's schools,
> I realized that my hosts, despite their material poverty, were
> far from victims. Instead, they were resourceful, persistent,
> and attuned to solutions to lift themselves out of poverty.
> The experience transformed me. I left committed to address
> social justice on a global scale.

When asked about how she defines this commitment, she says:

> To me, global citizenship is a natural expansion of how we
> have historically conceived of citizenship as loyalty to one's
> community, state, or country. In a global, interconnected
> world, our lives are integrally entwined with those of
> others across the globe – most of whom we will never
> have the opportunity to meet. Global citizenship is the
> notion that we each have the responsibility to consider
> how our lives, decisions, and actions impact others across
> our global community.

Today's gap students, particularly those who have immersed themselves in other cultures, echo Abigail's belief that when students encounter other cultures personally, rather than just in a classroom, they develop a stronger awareness of, and sense of responsibility toward, those from other walks of life. That development becomes an education in itself. Although most gap experiences broaden a world view and expand awareness of other ways of life, for this chapter we are focusing on the observations of those who ventured abroad. Of the gap year participants we surveyed, 69 percent volunteered, studied, worked or interned, and/or traveled abroad. The survey explored how their global experiences shaped their views of what it means to be a "citizen of the world."

The main benefits described by those we interviewed who had international experiences include:

- gaining an in-depth awareness of how people live in other cultures;
- developing a moral sensibility that transcends borders;
- understanding cultural interconnectedness and the impact of globalization;
- seeing one's own country from the perspective of others; and
- discovering what we have in common with others, regardless of culture.

A pre-requisite for developing these perspectives, they say, is the ability to have the attitude of a wanderer, rather than that of a tourist, and to see things in another country or culture through the eyes of its citizens.

The specific areas we explored in the survey and interviews included how gap experiences shaped awareness of what is going on in the world, in politics, and social issues. We asked if participants gained a better understanding of other countries, people, cultures, and ways of life because of their gap year. Additionally, we asked if the experiences allowed participants to develop a better understanding of international affairs and how America is perceived by others. We probed in our survey and interviews about the sources of support – emotional, practical, or financial – during the gap year. To look at one aspect of the longer term impact of global experiences, we asked if participants are in regular contact with non-U.S. citizens they met abroad. The interviews also touched on the similarities and differences between traditional study abroad programs and gap experiences.

We also asked about parents' perspectives as their sons and daughters went on global journeys and returned, having discovered more about themselves. A number of the parents, it turns out, had ventured out on global gap years or similar experiences themselves in years past.

Caroline Ivy

Caroline Ivy's reflections illustrate how gap experiences can bring to life the concept of what it means to be a citizen of the world, building on an American identity and recognizing the potential to make a difference. She shared with us an essay she wrote about experiences with children in an orphanage in Chile that had been set up by the government for children between the ages of three and twelve who had been abused by their parents. The excerpt below is from the essay, "Every Other Monday," that Caroline wrote for her college English class.

> Parent visiting days were every other Monday afternoon. You could tell whose parents were dead because they paid no attention to the door. The other children, the majority, stood in the hallway, watching that door for hours. Their parents never came, and every other Monday night an entire home of sexually abused children in Chile would go to bed crying. I had my reservations about working with abused children. I heard they could be difficult, demanding, even hostile, but I thought I was ready for the challenge. It was a sunny Thursday afternoon as I stood on the doorstep of 351 Calle Romeo, a large house with peeling white paint, naive enough to think I was prepared for the inevitable adventures that lay ahead.

Noting the hostility she perceived of the resident staff toward the children, Caroline writes about taking advantage of her time alone with them on a daily walk to get bread in the village.

> Every afternoon I would go on a walk with about ten children to buy bread. It was on these walks that I encouraged participation in all the real-life, kid activities they constantly missed out on. Out of the vigilant eye of the Tia [orphanage staff], we threw spitballs, climbed trees, chased dogs, and wrestled in the grass. I slipped them pesos as we passed the candy store and pretended to retie my shoes while I waited outside. I was always up for a footrace in the street and one extra jump from the highest bench in the park.

Caroline's essay, reflecting the difficulty she had in accepting the circumstances in which the orphans found themselves, must have been painful to write. One wonders if those who have read or heard it do not share her rage, but also a feeling of powerlessness. According to her mother, Amy, the extreme circumstances at this orphanage proved overwhelming and drove her daughter to find another orphanage for abused children up to three years old where she performed basic child care duties – ones that did not tear at her heart as much on a daily basis. She also had to negotiate finding another place to live when her placement with her host family did not prove suitable.

One trend that emerged from the participants we connected with is that students, like Caroline, emerge more aware of the world and social issues through gap year experiences even when they involved facing challenges or wrenching realities. Eighty-two percent of the gappers who went abroad saw themselves as more aware of these issues after their gap year than before. That broke down to 38 percent said they were much more aware, and 44 percent said they were somewhat more aware.

In interviews, gappers generally emphasized the importance of having an open mind, empathizing, and being willing to put themselves in someone else's shoes in order to gain in-depth perspective from an experience in another culture. This can be a different approach than simply being an American tourist in another land. The survey also asked gappers to compare their global awareness after their international experiences to that of their peers. Sixty-nine percent viewed themselves as more aware – 33 percent said they were much more aware and 36 percent said they were somewhat more aware than their peers after a gap year.

Caroline grew more aware through a real-world education on poverty that she gained in South America and that influenced what and how she learned back in the classroom at college.

> You have to get out into the world and experience all kinds of things to really learn. I get so frustrated in my classes with these rich city kids who have never left the country talking about poverty and despair. You can read all you want about these things, but it is not until you meet the people who are living in these conditions and really experience it first-hand that you can actually learn.

Caroline attended the University of New Hampshire where she was in the Social Work honors program pursuing a dual major in Social Work and International Affairs. She says that her gap year changed her perspective on education.

> My gap year experience definitely changed my attitude toward education. I realized that without an education I would be forever putting band-aids on people's problems. It is easy enough to work at a homeless shelter and serve food, but it is something more to understand why homelessness exists and how poverty and oppression affect the development of people. By getting a good education, I can advocate for people in need and try to solve the larger problems, instead of always just covering them with a temporary fix.

> I think the most important result of my gap year experience is the direction it provided me, something that will hopefully remain with me for the rest of my life. Now I am motivated and energized by what it is that I am passionate about – helping those in need, adventure, and travel. I wouldn't have known this if I had never taken a gap year. Now, I can't imagine spending my life any other way. This is not to say that I know exactly what it is that I want to do when I'm older. ... My gap year helped me figure out what my passions are, and from that I will began the process of figuring out what to do with my life. Hopefully it will be a process that will take my whole life.

Of at least equal importance is that Caroline developed a keen moral sensibility, what Martha Nussbaum, Professor of Law and Ethics at the University of Chicago, characterizes in *Frontiers of Justice* as an overwhelming desire "to produce, and live in, a world that is morally decent, a world in which all human beings have what they need to live a life worthy of human dignity."

Emma Impink

Emma Impink's experience working at a baboon rehabilitation center in South Africa represents yet another way in which gappers can become immersed, discover their passion, and find it difficult to see the world the same as they did before. Emma gained perspective on the complexity of social issues as she recognized there is usually more than one way to consider social problems or challenges, whether at home or abroad.

> In South Africa baboons are like a problem species so they're allowed to be shot by farmers, which is upsetting coming from the United States where we're more about the World Wildlife Fund. We see all these animals and are like 'Oh

I can't believe anybody wants to destroy them,' but it's a reality, you know. These baboons plunder the farmers' fields and the farmers are trying to make a living so, for the most part, it's that the baboons are a pest, but there are some who kill a little more vindictively. This is a constant underlying tension, this conflict between humans and animals as the humans encroach more on the animals' territory, but it's sort of an encroachment of necessity. So it was very complicated. It actually made me aware that there are always two sides to every issue, because we spent lots of time out in the field closely observing elephants and I felt an affinity with them. After spending so much time, you really learn to appreciate the subtleties of their behavior.

We asked gappers to rate the extent to which their experiences provided them with "a better understanding of other countries, people, and cultures and ways of living." Given a list of options, 94 percent of the overseas cohort ranked this as a prominent outcome (eight, nine, or ten on a scale of one to ten).

Julie Siwicky

Many international gappers relay that immersion in a culture and living with a host family leads to powerful bonds. It's not unusual to hear gappers talk about host family members as "my second mother," "my brother," or "my little sister." Julie Siwicky traveled to India and lived with a host family to discover that she had a common bond with people half way around the world. We asked her why she believes an international experience provided her with a broader understanding of other cultures.

Julie explained that she left her home in suburban Philadelphia for a gap year that began with travel in India as part of a Global Learning

Across Borders (GLAB) group. GLAB's mission is to "educate and inspire new generations of people to become responsible and committed global citizens in their local communities and beyond" with a focus on international cultural immersion programs. Her home stay in India led to an in-depth view of how others live and also to a realization of how much we are alike.

> Living in homestays in India really exposed me to lifestyles different from my own. Previous to my experience, I had heard about poor people living in 'one-room huts,' although I could never imagine just what this would be like. As it turned out, in India I lived with a family of three (husband, wife, and nine-month old boy) in a single room apartment for the better part of a month. Moreover, they spoke close to no English while I spoke close to no Tibetan (their language). Regardless, we were able to communicate with each other and became quite close. In a sense, I learned that all humans are the same on a basic level. On the other hand, I gained an appreciation for the extremely different experiences that humans have. These host parents had, in their youth, made a dangerous escape out of Chinese-occupied Tibet. I was baffled by the struggles they'd faced in their lives, especially compared to my life of relative comfort in suburban Philadelphia. Of course I learned a lot more about other countries, cultures, religions, etc. during my gap year, but what I learned from connecting with this host family sticks with me the most now.

Ben Ewing

The intensity of experiences living as part of a family abroad also is reflected in the words of Ben Ewing, based on his home stay in Cuzco, Peru.

I would say the most valuable part was the time when I wasn't a tourist, where I was living in this culture, living with this family who completely accepted me, and completely took me under their roof. I would go to their family weddings. I went to their Easter celebration, and the huge parades in downtown. I met cousins and grandchildren and friends of the family, and they took me to their camp spot up in the mountains and we went camping. It felt great. I feel like I have another family from a completely different background, completely different culture.

Malaka Refai

The number one answer to the question of the impact that gap years had on individuals – whether at home or abroad – was that they found more out about themselves. Many students, like Malaka Refai, found that journeys abroad can be a road to self-discovery.

Malaka found herself burned out when she entered Princeton University, so during her freshman year she began investigating gap years. Her goals were associated with learning in a different way.

To learn without having a grade attached to it, to move outside of the structures of academia, to meet real people from all different walks of life, and most of all build trust in myself. I love to learn but I was burnt out from standard teaching methods within the confines of the classroom. I also had spread myself way too thin during my first year of college working too much in theatre management and I needed to be somewhere else entirely.

As a Muslim with family roots in Egypt, Malaka found little initial support for her wide-ranging plan from her parents.

> My father laughed and my mother freaked out. My father thought I wasn't serious and he had an image of his daughter gallivanting around the world and not doing anything with her life. Mom didn't want her little girl to go since she believed the world to be too dangerous. I think she also feared I would never come back. Being pretty conservative Egyptian Muslims, the concept of letting their youngest and only daughter go off on her own was a pretty foreign one.

Her high school counselor also wasn't supportive, though one of her teachers who had taken a gap year while at Princeton was a great advocate. "After much convincing and planning, my father warmed up to the idea, as my mother continued to freak out. This was something I was going to do, and I think they saw my determination and went along with it."

Malaka's journey took her first to Egypt where she worked with two social workers in a shelter for street kids, boys who were five- to twelve-years-old. She then worked in Southern Chile in a bed and breakfast where she developed a love for Latin American culture. Her Spanish improved significantly when her Chilean friends took away her Spanish-English dictionary and made her develop her own vocabulary. Her fluency in Spanish actually became a barrier when she moved on to work on an organic farm in Ireland and was surrounded by English again and "couldn't understand a drop of what anyone was saying."

Her travels took her to a variety of places and different cultures, and she found a strong connection with people wherever she went.

> In Egypt, Chile, Ireland, England, and Germany I was welcomed with open arms by complete strangers. I learned so much about these cultures and ways of life I don't know where to start. In all these places I met such different people but I was so lucky and blessed because they were all kind, genuine people with amazingly big hearts.

Malaka returned to her studies with increased appreciation for structured learning, in part because she met people in her travels who knew so much more history than she did and asked her questions about the U.S. and its role in the world that she could not answer. Malaka's "time on," as she terms her gap year, also provided her with a basis for comparing her chosen path with those of her peers when she returned home. Her whirlwind of experiences caused her to feel redefined to the extent that she had problems sharing her experiences with those close to her. The disparity between her new self and the lives of her peers is captured in her account of a social occasion a few days after her return.

> I went to a music festival to see my brother and some of our friends play music. It was nice to go to the shore for this musical gathering, but I ran into a lot of people and I recall trying to play catch-up with them. It was in the middle of the summer and these people I was talking to were going on and on about all the drugs they've done so far and how much more they were planning on doing. This was the highlight of their time off. I am not one to judge any person's extra-curricular [activities], but I remember just being so happy that I could remember my experiences; that they were tangible and they were something I could look back on. I saw the path these people were on and I really knew that it was not the path I wanted to be on.

Perceptions of Americans Abroad

Another attribute of global citizenship we were curious about is what happens when a young person ventures abroad and learns how others perceive America and Americans – a perception that can be less then positive. We asked our gappers to rate, again on a scale of one to ten, the extent to which their experiences gave them a better understanding of how America is perceived by others. Eighty-one percent rated this as a strong impact of a gap year (eight, nine, or ten on a scale of one to ten).

Erin O'Neil

Erin O'Neil's gap year journey abroad led her to conclude that the world is interconnected even though sometimes Americans think "it's all about us."

Erin traces her interest in travel to a family trip she took during her equivalent of fifth grade. Erin and her twin sister were taught by their mother for twelve months as the family traveled around the U.S. and Canada in a minivan. She attributes her skepticism about formal education to this formative experience, where she found how much can be learned – albeit at the hands of a certified teacher like her mother – outside of the classroom and through travel. "I learned more during that trip about myself, my family, how others live, and the history of North America than I ever did in school. In fact, if I had it my way, I never would have gone back to school! When we re-entered the school system in Texas, we were far beyond our peers in terms of education and maturity level."

After a difficult senior year in high school, she felt she needed to get an idea of who she was outside of what she perceived at the time as the constraints of formal education. "I also had a strong desire to travel and do something different. I was tired of doing what everyone was expected to do in life." Her gap year include volunteering, serving, studying, and traveling abroad. She began in Providence, Rhode Island, at Brown University's summer school program where she took philosophy of law and creative non-fiction writing. She then participated in a program through the Institute for Cultural Ecology that took her to Hawaii to study dolphins and sea turtles, to Fiji to stay with a host family and work on an eco-tourism project for the village, and then to Australia to learn about history, culture, and geography. Then LEAPNOW took her to Guatemala, Costa Rica, and Honduras to participate in Spanish language immersion, service work, and travel. She invested time to travel and hike in Italy and visit Paris with friends before returning to the United States.

As a result of her journeys, Erin says she's "more empathetic than my peers. I look at everything in a global context and am probably more politically aware than my peers." Her experiences also gave her a broader perspective on American life.

> While part of me walked away thinking 'wow, we have it good here in America,' another part of me walked away thinking 'wow, we live in such a shell in America and take so much for granted.' I had the opportunity to live with people who were what we would consider the poorest of the poor. Living with them made me grateful for what I had, but seeing their smiles, their excitement at the slightest thing, and their sense of family, made me realize that we take a lot for granted in America. Yes, they were poor, but they were happy. They found a way to survive on what they had, and that was okay with them. They lived in far greater harmony with the land than we do. I also learned that people from other countries are much more geographically aware than

most Americans. Everyone seemed to know so much about America and what was going on in the world as a whole, even children. Yet, in America, many people can't even point out Fiji on a map.

Erin also sees her world view as setting her apart from her contemporaries, particularly her awareness of the interconnectedness between America and the rest of the world.

> I know something that set me apart from my peers when I returned was my global perspective. I learned that there is a whole world out there that's interconnected with everything we do. I learned that there are people in countries like Guatemala and Fiji, living lives entirely different from the ones that we are living in America and that doing even one little thing for them can make a big difference. I think Americans forget sometimes that there is an entire world out there and that it isn't all about us. Traveling around that world and staying with people was really a humbling experience.

When we last connected, Erin was a stay-at-home mom. She was doing legal work for a law firm, writing and preparing parole evaluations and parole prospectuses for inmates. When asked if she believes her year will have a lasting impact, she answers: "Definitely. My gap year gave me experiences I can't wait to share with my daughter."

Many gappers, like Erin, note that they have developed friendships that they never would have imagined without the gap experience. It's not unusual to hear "I have friends and places to stay in another part of the world." Thirty-five percent (representing a majority of those who went abroad) of gappers in our survey had remained in contact with non-U.S. citizens they met after their year away.

Gap Years and Study Abroad Experiences

We met a mother at St. John's College in Santa Fe, New Mexico, who asked whether there is a difference between a gap year and a study abroad experience. She asked a good question. Her son, it turns out, was about to go out on a gap experience, beginning with the National Outdoor Leadership School (NOLS). Her daughter had decided to forego a gap year for what she perceived as a "safer" option of a study abroad program sponsored by her university. Our survey results and those from other studies underscore that there are similarities between gap year and study abroad programs. The interviews we conducted with international gappers emphasize that there also are differences.

According to the website of St. John's University in New York City, a study abroad program can be defined as the opportunity to go to school in a different country where students "experience a different culture and their perspective is broadened through their daily interaction within a new environment." A program generally is tied to a college or university and frequently results in college credit. It generally requires some form of documentation from the experience – a paper, journal, or other product. The Institute of International Education (IIE), a not-for-profit organization founded in 1919 to offer "experienced international education and training" programs, conducts research on study abroad trends. It reports that more than 270,000 students have gone abroad in recent years, representing a four-fold increase in students abroad over the last three decades.

Another organization that focuses on study abroad experiences is the International Institute for Educational Studies (IES). IES, based in Chicago, was established in 1950 and today offers college students international program opportunities in thirty-one countries around the world. An IES study of 3,400 alumni of study abroad programs found that such programs are "usually a defining moment in a young person's life and continue to impact the participant's life for years after the experience." This is a theme we have also heard from gap students about their experiences, whether they focused on studying or other activities abroad.

In considering similarities between gap and study abroad sessions, the findings of the IIE survey corroborated those of our survey, specifically for those whose experiences included one or more overseas components. Research finds that:

- 82 percent of study abroad alums replied that the experience helped them develop a more sophisticated way of looking at the world;

- 94 percent of gap alums who traveled overseas said that they gained "a better understanding of other countries, people, cultures and ways of living"; and

- 63 percent said a major impact of study abroad experiences is that they influenced their decision to expand or change academic majors.

In an IIE survey, 23 percent still maintain contact with host-country friends compared with the 35 percent of the gap year alums who were in regular contact with non-U.S. citizens they met during their gap year.

While there are elements of study abroad programs that overlap with the experiences of gap year alums, such as those noted above, the interviews we conducted point to elements that set gap year experiences apart. In a few cases, we interviewed students who participated in both study abroad programs while in college and who also did gap years overseas on their own. One distinction is that while study abroad programs generally provide the same structure for all participants, gap experiences tend to be more individual. As the *Harvard Crimson* staff noted in an editorial on gap years, an experience tied to an academic institution and organized by professionals may "offer students less growth, individual initiative, spontaneous travel, and heedless soul-searching."

Parker Stevens

Parker Stevens shared with us an ambitious gap year itinerary that illustrates the variety as well as the depth of what a gapper can experience over the span of a year. When we heard from Parker, he was studying abroad in Dar es Salaam, Tanzania, an indication of the fluency in other cultures he developed during his gap journeys.

Parker was one of the many gappers who had worked hard in high school and believed that, if he went straight to college, he would "burn out pretty quickly." He took his lead from a friend who was considering gap year options. "The more I looked into what was available, the more I realized that I wanted to take some time for myself before college."

Here is Parker's gap year itinerary in his words. His journey began with "South Africa through Travelers Worldwide (the program in South Africa that they set us up with is called African Global Academy); September-October 2004. Here I took a course on African wildlife and conservation. We were a small group and lived in tents on an olive farm outside of two game reserves. We would have lectures in the morning and some sort of practical experience in the afternoon (i.e. hikes, game drives, game counts, tracking, etc.). Then I went to Costa Rica through School of the World; November 2004 where I took a Spanish course and learned to surf."

The next segment of his gap year was in "New Zealand through Wildlands Studies (an extension of University of California, Santa Barbara) for six weeks; January-mid February 2005. I was with a group of fifteen amazing people road tripping around New Zealand. We would camp out in beautiful locations and learn about animal behavior, ecology of NZ, and Maori culture. It was easily one of the best experiences of my life." An additional experience was in "Fiji through the Institute for Cultural Ecology; February-March 2005. Here I lived with a family in a small coastal village. Five years before, the area in front of the village was severely over-fished, so they turned it into a marine protected area. We did surveys on the reef to determine if the protection helped the fish populations recover."

Parker then was in "Australia on my own to travel around: April, 2005" and then "back to New Zealand with Live New Zealand; May 2005. This program was fantastic. I lived in a studio apartment with another volunteer and worked at an elementary school. I was a teacher's assistant in a second grade class. The school was very relaxed and had a strong focus on Maori culture. I was in Wellington, which quickly became my favorite city in the world. It is very laid back, the people are wonderful, and there is great music every night."

Parker draws a direct connection between his global experiences and his chosen course of study, environmental science, that led him to Africa and study at the University of Dar es Salaam:

> Before I left I had already applied and been accepted to college, but I think that having a break beforehand changed a lot. I was so burnt out after high school, but my gap year really rejuvenated me and got me excited about learning again. In high school, I was so frustrated that I couldn't choose what I wanted to study, and when I graduated I really

didn't know what I was interested in. I chose a few different types of programs (environmental, teaching, language, etc.) so that I could explore my personal interests. I really gravitated towards the environmental programs even though I had never really thought of myself as an environmentalist. After my gap year I realized that was what I am truly passionate about, and now I am studying environmental science and engineering.

A question emerged in considering the difference between study abroad programs and gap experiences: If fostering global citizenship is a goal, are school-sponsored study abroad programs more likely to serve this end better than individualized gap year programs? As a pragmatic consideration, students (and their parents) who are seeking course credit would tend to favor school-sponsored programs. There also are opportunities in some more individualized gap year opportunities to get both college credit and financial aid. In weighing the relative advantage of each approach, another difference that might be considered was summarized by the mother we met at St. John's College in Santa Fe. Study abroad might be the "safer" alternative, but relatively unknown gap years take an individual who is somewhat of a risk-taker.

Study abroad programs generally involve American students' living and traveling together, while gap students often spend time traveling alone, in homestays, or living with people from other cultures or backgrounds. Study abroad programs often involve the relative security of having an adult-supervised American home base, while individual gap opportunities can involve being vulnerable in a foreign culture as a condition of learning. School-sponsored programs can reinforce the primacy of pursuing academic credit compared to a more experiential gap approach that comes through volunteering or working overseas.

Differences also come up in interviews with gappers who have done both school-sponsored study abroad programs and individual gap years. In these cases, there was a clear preference for the latter, with an emphasis on the need to maximize the kind of learning that one gets outside of an academic setting, not looking for school credit, but focusing on the experience itself.

Lucas Hildebrand

One gap alum who had the hands-on opportunity to compare gap and study abroad experiences was Lucas Hildebrand. Lucas's mother, Cindy, took the initiative in suggesting a gap year to her son. He had experienced problems in high school, especially with math, due to a diagnosed perceptual impairment. Lucas had already been accepted to a couple of colleges but took his mother's advice. He requested deferrals and began his gap year at the age of seventeen working in the Redwoods National Park in California. He set off in the second half of his gap year with his best friend to work as a volunteer on an organic farm in Australia, part of the WWOOF (World Wide Opportunities On Organic Farms) network. He also found work at a hostel at a nearby beach. Cindy provided perspective on Lucas's gap experience compared to a study abroad college program he participated in later during which he returned to Australia. She observed that during his study abroad it was difficult for Lucas to be serious about his studies because the program appeared to be "more of a party time." More importantly, and unlike his gap year experience, Lucas "didn't have to fend for himself."

Tourists vs. Wanderers

It could be that when Americans travel in groups overseas, they are more likely to behave as tourists than trying to see a foreign culture or country through the eyes of their hosts. That may lead to a perception that they are resistant to new surroundings and even disrespectful. As Silvia Montiglio, associate professor of classics at the University of Wisconsin (Madison), reminds us in *Wandering in Ancient Greek Culture*, there is a difference between "tourists" and "wanderers." The former collects facts as curiosities – "not in their meaning with the system of the foreign culture, but in their exoticism with respect to his own cultural system."

Amanda Nooter

Amanda Nooter was inclined to view her experiences in Greece, where she was volunteering with The Silva Project, through the lens of her host country's culture and customs instead of as a tourist. The Silva Project is a non-profit organization in Corfu, Greece which is dedicated to preserving a certain breed of horse called the Skyrian. Volunteers are involved in rescuing animals that have been abused, working in a riding school, or serving on an organic kiwi farm that the organization owns. Here's how Amanda described her experiences with Greek Easter on the island of Corfu from a distinctly non-American viewpoint, excerpted from emails sent home. Amanda explains that Easter celebrations go on for four days and the highlight, from her perspective, was a ritual of pot-smashing.

On Saturday we all woke up fairly early and walked into town to witness the famous Corfu tradition of smashing pots. At 11 am exactly every family in town perches their personalized clay pots on their window sills and then drops them onto the street. Hordes of people come to watch but of course there is room left for the pots to drop. It was really exciting to watch – families compete to have the biggest and most elaborately decorated pots and every time one falls there is a lot of cheering. Some of the pots had water in them and when they landed it sounded like a balloon popping. Afterwards I picked up some of the shards of clay to keep. Saturday night we walked into town yet again to witness the 'happy' parades (at this point Christ had been resurrected) and an amazing fireworks show. Everyone was walking around with lit candles and the effect was breathtaking. Traditionally everyone is supposed to fast all day and then break the fast at midnight with a special soup of pig/lamb (I can't remember which one) intestines. ...I'm still not entirely sure why they smash the pots but I think it has something to do with a passage from the Bible. In any case that was certainly the best part and I feel so lucky to have been here to see it.

Stephanie Horn

For some gappers, being an American abroad can lead to stark realizations about how others might generalize about our culture and citizens. Stephanie Horn attended Oxford Tutorial College where some of her most memorable experiences occurred outside her intensive tutorial sessions. These included heated discussions around the invasion of Iraq with students from a variety of backgrounds, including Jews, Muslims and "Brits" who had been gappers themselves. Stephanie was astonished by the animosity exemplified in a debate at the Oxford Union where it was resolved (favorably) that "The United States is the biggest threat to peace in the world." She found the experience to be humbling and one that led her to question everything she thought she knew and understood. Her term at Oxford was fundamental to her political awareness. "It changed my whole perspective on life."

Experiencing Anti-Americanism

Carol Madison Graham was Executive Director of the US UK Fulbright Commission from 2002-2006 and is author of *Coping with Anti-Americanism: A Guide to Getting the Most Out of Studying Abroad*. We asked Carol for advice she would offer to students who experience anti-American sentiments.

> Even students who regularly follow international events are surprised to find that dislike of the United States and Americans is as common, and possibly more common, than positive views. Americans overseas used to tell themselves that anti-Americanism was really aimed at the U.S. government and that overall the American public is liked. In some places this still holds true but over the years general dislike of Americans themselves has greatly increased. Fat, arrogant, uncultured, ignorant, and protective of a way of life that is polluting the planet. These are some of the stereotypes that are attributed to Americans by others and especially by young people. Often the same young people who wear jeans, learn English, and eat big Macs.

Gap year students cannot eliminate a stereotyped view of Americans but they can challenge it by mastering the language and culture of their host culture as well as U.S. culture and history. They will then be in a strong position to listen to, explain, and discuss distorted impressions of the United States and Americans.

Adam Haigler

For some students, emerging as a global citizen is a process of awareness and reflection that occurs over time and develops with repeated immersion in other cultures. We were interested recently in our son Adam's observations about being an American abroad during a recent trip he took to Peru, seven years after his inaugural gap experience in Costa Rica.

Like many gappers, Adam set out on his first journey to Central America as a wide-eyed, 18-year old excited to explore the world. He ventured out with a structured program called Global Routes through which he spent three-and-a-half months in the mountain village of Oratorio. His time included a home stay and his subsequent "adoption" by his host family. Also, like many gappers, Adam's instinct when he saw the relative disparity in resources between his host village and his life in America was to see how to help out. While in Costa Rica during his first visit, he wrote the following e-mail:

In my school there is absolutely nothing. They are only maybe fifty textbooks issued by the government. What I propose to you guys is to see if there is any interest in a book fund with family, friends, PTA, stewardship committee at church, whatever, to help out these kids with a box of

English-Spanish dictionaries and English and Spanish books. I think it would help continue the English learning process long after Global Routes leaves. On Friday an eighteen-year old cousin of mine told me that when we leave, he won't learn anymore English. I don't want this to be the case.

Adam also noted that there is a lack of government funding in Costa Rica for education as the cost for one student to go to high school was $125 a year. When he returned to the United States, he stayed in contact with his new family. He raised a scholarship fund sufficient to support eight students to move on to high school from the elementary *escuela* where he taught. On one of his three trips back to Oratorio since his gap year, he met with the local school board and tried to make sure that the funds were being used for the intended purpose –"to support the educational aspirations of the children of poor coffee farmers." It turned out the funding resulted in some controversy. Some people approached Adam and advised that they believed the school board wasn't being fair in their selection of scholarship recipients. They said that the board members were favoring their own family and friends.

Fast forward seven years to when Adam traveled to Peru for one of a number of global experiences since his first time in Costa Rica. Below is an entry from his travel blog that provides a retrospective view of his efforts to help the school in Oratorio.

I've had many varied experiences in the developing world now, mostly Central America, that demonstrated to me the negative and positive potential for intercultural exchange – especially between two financially disparate cultures. Primarily, I saw how flowing thousands of dollars into a small rural village for a do-gooder scholarship and library fund could cause a controversy among the residents, even with the purest of intentions. Since then I've been much more careful about financial charity and have thought long and hard about how I can most effectively act as a global citizen and an ambassador of my country. I've come to the conclusion (far from final) that the best I can do if I intend to spend time in the developing world is to treat people like people. This is the problem I see most among tourists – not seeking conversations, experiences, or interactions with anyone but other tourists which I believe can have inadvertent negative impacts on the host country. ... Conversely, if I show through my words and actions that I am interested in the people whose place I am visiting, I am demonstrating solidarity with the people there, at least a little bit, and am thus taking a small step towards a more egalitarian world. ... To be continued.

We asked Adam by email if he recalled the earlier impulse of his 18-year old self to raise funds with the intention of helping his adopted friends and family in Costa Rica. We also asked about the nature of the controversy he refers to in his blog that he perceives as a result of his early well-intentioned philanthropy. And we asked what advice he'd give to his younger self and other gappers setting out in the world with a goal of giving to others.

Here is his initial response when reading his email from years ago which seems to him now that "they were written by a different person":

Wow, it's like looking in a mirror, except I see a naive little guy on the other end. I was also less cynical then and more willing to help – but maybe not as wise to the game I was a part of. I've got A LOT of new perspective on this subject after working with Threads of Peru [a not-for-profit organization focused on education about the Andean people and their textile traditions] but at this point it's not well-organized – just scattered journal entries. At the moment I'm fighting the magnetism of the internet cafes so that I can continue being present in Peru.

We know Adam's reflections will evolve over the years along those of other gappers who would like to view themselves as emerging global citizens. It may be an idea for parents, programs, and gappers, themselves, to hang on to emails and other remembrances from international global experiences over time to more systematically document the nature of this evolution. To be continued.

Parents' Insights

Through the interviews, parents emerge as one of the most original sources of insight on the impact of gap years on their children's global awareness. In many cases, the parents of gappers who have chosen overseas opportunities have had international experience themselves, in travel, in work, or in volunteering. A number took gap years or had similar investments of time themselves. It could be that a family's cumulative experience helps set the stage for some gap year students to have positive outcomes from their time overseas.

Cory Masters

In Charmaine Masters' case, the family's living in Bermuda set the stage for daughter Cory's global gap year. Charmaine says her family has been global in its point of view as well as their places of residence. She was not surprised when her daughter looked to foreign climes for her gap year. Cory had a difficult time in school due to an auditory disability and, though she won awards in a new day school that was a good match for her, she wasn't satisfied that her performance matched her potential. She couldn't see herself going to school right away for four more years. Instead, she "wanted to get her hands dirty" and challenge herself in settings outside of the classroom. She also was interested in trying out new things and immersing herself in unfamiliar experiences. Cory was a born risk-taker.

Once her parents helped out by purchasing health insurance, Charmaine says that they were proud to witnesses Cory's travels to Southeast Asia, Pakistan, and India. In India, Cory worked in the Home for the Destitute and Dying and proved her mettle when the young men in her group couldn't bear up under the burden. She and her group witnessed first-hand the challenges of traveling alone on trains in Pakistan and the travails of the poor. In one case, a young mother in Thailand who had become a prostitute to feed her children threw herself off a ferry rather than being taken to jail.

When Cory returned from her time away, she was much more contemplative, according to Charmaine. She wouldn't have extraneous things in her room and was kept up at night by what she had experienced. She translated her gap year mental pictures into vivid photos she had taken and through the letters and e-mails she had written during the year to share with family and friends. Her sensitivity to the plight of others and growing self-awareness during the year has left an imprint that has led to an ability to express herself as an artist.

Regardless of whether parents have spent time abroad themselves, there is little doubt that parents play a pivotal role in supporting gappers – first, in planning, then during the experience itself, and finally in assisting with the transition back home. Support from home during gap years can be especially important for those who go overseas. Our survey asked: *How important was each of the following sources of emotional and/or practical support during your gap year?* The ranking of sources of support, based on the average of gapper rankings, clearly demonstrates the importance of family and friends. Family and friends were ranked at the top with 7.6 on a ten-point scale, closely followed by "peers in my area or program" with 7.56.

Lily Hollister

Chip Hollister's support for, and perspective on, daughter Lily's gap experience may be unique in some respects. As a practicing psychologist, Chip was adamant that his daughter, Lily, would not "paint by the numbers" when it came to her future. When she began to take control of her gap year plan, he took the position that "learning for learning's sake" was more important than just aiming for a college degree as a credential. Lily's gap year focused on developing facility in Spanish, so she went to Costa Rica for language study and to learn about the culture. She immersed herself in native dances such as the Salsa and Meringue.

Lily's dad has seen the influence of her experiences in greater self-awareness, love of reading, and above all her self-directedness. Critical to all of these was her ability to "see herself through the different lenses" of another culture. At the conclusion of her gap year, Lily considered returning to the United States but, like a number of gappers, she experienced a severe reverse culture shock. She decided to return to Costa Rica for college. By registering as an international student, Lily is able to pursue her college education at a fraction of what it would cost in the United States. True to her growing sense of responsibility, as a nineteen-year old she obtained employment as a certified TESOL (Teacher of English to Speakers of Others Languages). She balances her college and work schedules and still has had the opportunity to pursue her passion in dance – becoming, in the words of her proud father, an exquisite Latin American dancer.

Andrew Lauch

Parental legacy also can act as a powerful motivator for gappers' choosing the adventure and embracing the risks of travel abroad. Andrew Lauch's father, Dennis, had been a Peace Corps volunteer in Colombia in the 1970s. Three decades later, his son was headed on a gap year, starting in India. Andrew Lauch's gap year took him to Bangalore, India, where he worked with elementary-school age children at a boarding school. The school was established by the George Foundation specifically to provide educational opportunities for the "poorest of the poor." The Foundation was established in 1995 to "work toward poverty eradication in India, promote environmental health, and strengthen democratic institutions and values in developing countries." Andrew was looking for an experience that would get him "outside of his comfort zone" – a phrase heard repeatedly from those we interviewed, especially those who worked, volunteered, or studied abroad. Andrew found his own zone when he became responsible for a roomful of children for three and a half months. He also came to sense that "being part of something bigger than myself" is one of the attributes associated with becoming a global citizen.

Among the things Andrew had to manage was how to balance his desire to be a friend with the need to be an authority figure. He was able to make a direct contribution, he felt, to the wellbeing of his charges and continued to be involved with them, as seen below in this blog entry from his second visit.

> Well the children have grown physically, that was anticipated, but one thing that I was unable to predict before arriving the second time was how much they would have grown mentally, both intellectually and emotionally. I was so pleased to see how all of the children in grades two through five have become so much more grown-up since I last saw them, whether it is with their level of sports skill, or their ability academically. They all seem to be progressing just as they should and it is such a joy to be able to watch them become individuals. ...I worked with many of the grades, reading with them and exposing them to more books in the library in the hopes of spawning an interest in reading and in books in general. ...I really cannot sufficiently express the enjoyment I receive at being a contributing part of this organization. Returning to volunteer has cemented a certain aspect of ownership for me here and I feel so at home in such a warm and very familiar environment.

When he returned to attend Pitzer College in Claremont, California, Andrew noticed that his thirst for learning far outstripped that of his peers. So he took the initiative to transfer, first to a local community college and eventually to the University of California at Berkeley where he graduated with a major in developing world studies. He attributes his time in India not only with the decision to pursue this major, but with a commitment to pursue graduate studies at the London School of Economics.

Andrew's parents saw the experience as transformative in that he came back much more mature, self-directed, and ready to go to college. As a former Peace Corps volunteer, his father, Dennis, understood much of what Andrew went through while in India and when he returned. He understood, for instance, that there is value in adversity, risk-taking, and spending time alone. On the latter point, Dennis commented that Andrew enjoyed his time the most when other Americans were not around.

Andrew is another student who experienced reverse culture shock to a degree that almost led him to return to India as soon as he got back. Dennis's Peace Corps tour helped the father to relate to his son's experiences, where Andrew's other friends and acquaintances could not. Andrew feels his parents' pride in him and he has a sense (that they share) that he can go anywhere, be by himself, but not feel alone. Andrew, in other words, sees himself as a global citizen, not alone anywhere in the world.

Sareeta Ramdial

A number of our parent-child interviews reveal the correlation between parents' experiences (as in the case of Dennis Lauch's experience in the Peace Corps) and their child's openness to work and study overseas. A singular example of a parent's influence can be seen in the case of Sareeta Ramdial. Sareeta was born on a kibbutz in Israel where her mother, Beverly Hugo, and her Hindu father, were working. She attended high school in Portland, Maine. Her mother became known for hiking the Appalachian Trail at age forty-eight. Nicknamed "Maine Rose," she wrote *Women and Thru-Hiking on the Appalachian Trail: Practical Advice from Hundreds of Women Long Distance Hikers* (1999), based on her experiences. It was Maine Rose who suggested a gap year option when Sareeta said she didn't know what she wanted to do in college. Her daughter applied and was accepted at Lawrence University in Appleton, Wisconsin, was granted a deferral, and launched into her gap year plan.

Sareeta's journey over two gap years included time working in an Australian boarding school as a teacher's assistant; working as a WWOOF (World Wide Opportunities On Organic Farms) volunteer for room and board in New Zealand; studying Spanish in Salamanca, Spain, and living with a host family; and working with the Monteverde Institute in Costa Rica. Sareeta kept in touch with those back home primarily through post cards or letters. She made a special point of communicating with the Director of Admissions at Lawrence, which became particularly useful when she requested a second deferral to extend her gap experience.

With the encouragement and enthusiastic support of her mother, but to the bewilderment of relatives and teachers who feared that she would not return to school, Sareeta took advantage of what she terms "the freest time in your life." She learned how to accommodate different belief systems, which she says is critical to learning cultural sensitivity, and found that the reciprocity in learning and sharing made her much more outgoing and less self-conscious. Working with underprivileged women in Costa Rica, for instance, she valued the opportunity to interact directly with clients in women's circle activities and serve as a confidant to those who shared intimate, difficult details of their lives.

One of Sareeta's insights into her gap year experience is that, "in order to know yourself, you have to be by yourself." We heard this from a number of other gappers we interviewed, almost as a corollary to "being outside your comfort zone." She welcomed the chance to "buck the American stereotype," holding herself accountable by acting as a guest in the countries as a wanderer rather than as a tourist. Upon her return to college, Sareeta found herself more at home with international students at Lawrence University as she participated in and eventually led the International Club. An excerpt from a university press release on the class arriving on campus attests to how Sareeta's gap years made her stand out from the other 398 students in her freshman class.

> As a senior at Deering High School in Portland, Maine, Sareeta Ramdial knew she wanted to attend Lawrence University. She just opted for the long way of getting here. More than 27 months and 35,000 miles later, Ramdial will finally reach the Appleton campus on Friday. Since graduating from high school in 1998, Ramdial has earned enough credit for a degree in life experiences. Born on a kibbutz in Israel, Ramdial, 20, has already seen more of the world than some space shuttle pilots. Her odyssey from Maine to Maine Hall over the past two years has involved more address changes than an FBI informant in the witness protection program.

The press release traces Sareeta's gap year journey, including in New Zealand where she "roamed the countryside, tending to emus, picking asparagus and harvesting kiwis for a local winery."

Sareeta's mom passed away in 2001. A part of her legacy is Sareeta's certainty that her mom knew that, as a result of her time away, she would be fine. There is not a day that passes, Sareeta says, when she does not think about her two years as the "highlight of her life" and remembers her mom.

******

Gap Year Survey Findings Summary

- *Do many gappers include international experiences in a gap year?* Of the gap year participants we surveyed, 69 percent volunteered, studied, worked or interned, and/ or traveled abroad.

- *What are the benefits of international gap year experiences?* Gap alums report that benefits include: gaining an in-depth awareness of how people live in other cultures; developing a moral sensibility that transcends borders; understanding cultural interconnectedness and the impact of globalization; seeing one's own country from the perspective of others; and discovering what we have in common with others, regardless of culture.

- *Do gappers who go abroad as part of their gap year emerge with greater global awareness?* In the survey, 82 percent of the gappers who went abroad saw themselves as more aware of these issues after their gap year than before (38 percent said they were "much more aware"; 44 percent said they were "somewhat more aware").

- *Do international gappers gain* "a better understanding of other countries, people, and cultures and ways of living?" Given a list of options, 94 percent of the overseas cohort ranked this as a prominent outcome (eight, nine, or ten on a scale of one to ten).

- *Do international gappers gain an understanding of how America is perceived by others in the world?* Eighty-one percent of those responding to the survey rated this as a strong impact of a gap year (eight, nine, or ten on a scale of one to ten).

- *What are sources of emotional and/or practical support for gappers abroad?* Survey respondents ranked family and friends at the top (7.6 on a ten-point scale) followed closely by "peers in my area or program" (7.56 on a ten-point scale).

Tips

Refer to programs and other gap year websites for up-to-date information on

- *Airfare and other travel*
- *Communication (phones, Internet, etc)*
- *Visas*
- *Safety, etc.*

The U.S. Department of State Travel Tips website in a good resource: http://travel.state.gov/travel/tips/tips_1232.html

Chapter Eight

GAPPERS LOOK IN THE MIRROR

"A semester off made me confront myself for the first time ever because I've always had someone else to interact with. I've never actually had to face myself and who I was and who I wanted to be and what direction I wanted to go in my life."

– Louis Lobel

There is a consensus among most gap year alums, counselors, parents, and college admissions officers that gappers return from their experiences more mature, with greater self-confidence, and generally more prepared for college life. Because we have heard this so often, it seems important to provide some depth to this common observation by asking alums to reflect on how much gap experiences contributed to their personal growth. What do they see when they look in the mirror?

The answer, in large part, is found in the words of the young adults who have discovered their own voices, many of whom have been heard in previous chapters. When they reflect on their experiences, they relay a sense of accomplishment and seem to have developed an internal anchor that secures them when they arrive on, or return to, campus.

When we asked about the most important outcomes of their gap years, the top answer was that it "gave them a better sense of who they are as a person."

This response is not surprising to Markus Naugle and Laura Wheelock, who are co-founders of Magic Carpet Rides, a not-for-profit organization dedicated to sharing what they describe as a global classroom. Their programs integrate immersion in other cultures with community service and natural exploration. (Yes, the organization's title is tied to the Steppenwolf song of the same name that was originally released in 1968.) Both world travelers, Markus has visited sixty countries and Laura had been to sixteen countries before her tenth birthday. Particularly related to the aspect of self-discovery, Markus believes that immersion in a new culture is "the most powerful mirror for personal reflection we know."

Most of the gap alums we connected with would agree. They describe the person they were prior to their gap year as different from the one who re-applied or applied to different schools afterwards, if applications were part of their plan. They see themselves in the mirror of their own experience as having undergone growth in the depth of their introspection and the breadth of their world view.

Jackie Levine

One way that gappers say they develop self-knowledge is realizing an integrated relationship between contributing to others and their own growth. This is reflected, for example, in the words of Jackie Levine who served as a City Year corps member in Roxbury, Massachusetts.

> Every day I was touched by something that happened. I especially bonded with a kindergartner named A.J. He was born addicted to cocaine and has been in and out of foster

homes his whole life. A.J. didn't respond well to authority or teachers. However, he really listened to me. We quickly formed a close relationship and I became his one-on-one tutor. I spent many days working on his speech, reading, and social skills. By the end of my year with A.J., he was a completely new kid. He was more mature and social and able to listen and follow directions. A.J. had gone through more things during his young life than I had experienced in twenty years. Although he had seen and experienced things that no one should have to go through, he was always happy and energetic. He taught me to see the good in people and to believe in myself and others. A.J. was forced to grow up quickly, and I have a lot of faith that he will be a successful member of society as he grows up. I think about him often and all of the lessons that he unknowingly taught me.

Jackie offers an example of how the tutor learned more about herself as she saw the personal growth reflected in her kindergarten pupil. She was able to specify the improvements that she saw as well, defining growth as a learner in terms of A.J.'s ability to listen and to follow directions. His optimistic outlook, seeing the good in others, for instance, was no doubt in part because of the attention that Jackie paid to him and the confidence she had that he could improve his skills and succeed. (Many top educators will report that there is a reciprocal aspect to teaching – that tutors learn as much or more from their students over time than they are able to transfer. This generally is associated with a more experienced and proficient teacher rather than the novice who may rely on one-way lectures as their natural classroom default.)

As indicated by our survey results and interviews, the gains associated with a gap year are generally not tied to résumé-driven, extrinsically-motivated purposes associated with the college admissions process. For example, Emma Impink, who bonded as seen in earlier chapters with her baboons in South Africa, gained insight into what it means to focus on solving problems in the real world as a path of self-discovery. As she says about her school experience, "I was really frustrated with thinking so much about myself. The past twelve years of my school career were just entirely self-centered. It was all about me, and especially the last push with the college application process which is completely selling yourself. And I was just so sick of writing about me." Having a gap year provided Emma with a new venue for discovery of herself outside of school, lessons that persisted throughout her gap year experience.

> I was part of three different programs [during my gap year], all of which were completely not about myself. I was completely on my feet, problem solving, doing all kinds of stuff where it was definitely not about me. It was really nice to get to know myself in an outside-of-school setting because, for so long, the only way I've known me is in school. School was my primary way of identifying myself, and where I thought I came from. So being outside of that and being with other people and not in a classroom was really fantastic.

Gaining a better understanding of oneself might be compared to trying to focus on a source of light in darkness; it is a physical fact that we see points of light better in such conditions using our peripheral vision. Similarly, a lot of the self-knowledge that comes during a gap year experience is gained while gappers are busy doing something rather than focusing on themselves – working as a tutor (as in Jackie's case) or an assistant in animal rehabilitation (as with Emma).

Self-Awareness

Kate Doyne

Another example of growing self-awareness coming out of giving to others is seen in Kate Doyne's experience as a Habitat for Humanity volunteer in Asia and South America as part of the LEAPNOW program. A number of questions in the interviews invited responses related to self-awareness. We asked Kate, for example, if alums gained skills, knowledge, or other abilities that they believe have contributed or will contribute to success or satisfaction in work or a career. When answering this question, Kate noted the impact of her experiences on her desire to become a teacher, citing how she learned to have a more open mind when immersed in new experiences. She also emphasizes the importance of communication, especially nonverbal communication, with her discovery that wherever she was in the world, "everyone smiles back when I smile."

Spending Free Time After a Gap Year

Another question that surfaced observations about the connection between gap year experiences and the development of self-awareness was about how respondents spent free time afterwards. We offered examples such as reading, writing, watching TV, music, food you prefer to eat, hobbies, exercise, and engaging in 'risky behaviors' such as drugs, or drinking too much. Kate exemplified many others interviewees in assessing her personal growth by comparing her post-gap year behavior with her peers. She said that afterwards she preferred spending time doing things she was interested in as opposed to what others wanted her to do. For example, her love of dance that was part of her self-discovery made her unapologetic about immersing herself in the movement and rhythm of African dancing after she returned from her gap year.

Allowing herself to make such choices with a clear sense of personal priorities led Kate to conclude, in a statement full of self-awareness and humility, that because of her experiences she became a person she is proud of – "a happy child, motivated, and excited about school." She describes herself as happier because she believes she became more complete and a confident self-learner through the gap year journey.

Kate's account of her gap year would not be properly concluded without also noting her answer to the question: *Do you believe your gap experience has had an impact on your relationships with your family or friends?* Kate shared the story of her younger sister, Maggie, who took a gap year right out of high school, traveling to Nepal where she started an orphanage and a non-profit organization that raises funds to support her work (www.blinknow.org). The maturity that Kate developed as a result of her experience inspired Maggie and will likely inspire all of their future students.

Thomas Czerwinski

Thomas Czerwinski's story represents the sentiments of numerous gappers we interviewed who reflect that their experiences helped bring out the essence of who they are as individuals. In Thomas's case, a short stint at a military academy right out of high school taught him what he did not want in his college experience, leaving him in the lurch when it came to how he would spend the remainder of his year. He was able to secure a position in a City Year program in Boston where he was put in a leadership position.

At age eighteen he found himself managing a team of fourteen City Year corps members. Most of them were older than he and, in keeping with the City Year philosophy, were from a variety of educational and socioeconomic backgrounds. Thomas said that the experience changed his personal life priorities: his focus moved away from prestige, status, and career toward community service. He found that, when it came to espousing the cause of diversity, he had to "walk the talk" in dealing with his City Year team.

The work of the team in a Boston area charter school required that Thomas develop management skills in planning and executing projects. During this time he learned about the importance of leadership in looking at both successes and failures as a medium of a team's learning.

Thomas's experience led to his informal and formal advising of younger students when he returned to school at Emory University in Atlanta, later serving as a residence counselor. He learned along the way that often the questions we ask of each other can influence others' behaviors. For example, when he had the opportunity to talk with students who were wondering about their life direction, he would ask the question integral to his City Year experiences, "Where are you going to do your service year?" His experience taught him that this question could be an eye-opener for those who sought his counsel compared to the one many are expecting: "Where are you going to college?" His exposure to inner-city challenges and its impact on the lives of the charter school students during City Year led Thomas to major in public policy as an undergraduate and to obtain a master's degree at the University of Texas's LBJ School of Public Policy.

A number of gap year parents have told us that they have enjoyed the reactions of their colleagues who routinely ask the "Where is your son or daughter going to college?" question. When they respond that John or Julie is not attending school next year, they can receive reactions ranging from surprise to curiosity to an occasional look of common understanding as they explain the gap year option. Some of these parents are now opting to pre-empt the college conversation by asking, "*Why* is John or Julie going to college next year?" Or even "So has John or Julie considered doing a gap year?"

These parents report that just posing an alternative question can open the door to options for learning outside the classroom that have helped gappers understand their strengths in specific, behavioral ways as they look in the mirror.

Growth In Competency Terms

One framework for capturing gappers' self-awareness comes from the respondents who ranked the eight competencies (SHL's Great Eight) in terms of their development as a result of their gap year and the contribution of the competencies to their success post-gap year. As we reported in the chapter on working and careers, the top three competencies gappers report developing are Leading and Deciding (making decisions when faced with challenges), Adapting and Coping (developing confidence and resilience), and Supporting and Cooperating (relating well to those with diverse backgrounds).

As noted earlier in the discussion of cross-cultural comparison with UK gap year alums, these competency areas correspond to the top skills identified by UK grads (from among the 15,000 respondents to the Hobsons Survey). Our hypothesis that there would be congruence between the U.S. and UK samples, based on their common experience of travel and/or volunteer work, appears to have been sustained.

In our interviews, we asked the respondents to provide examples of why and how they grew in self-awareness through developing abilities in the areas of Leading and Deciding, Adapting and Coping, and Supporting and Cooperating.

Leading and Deciding

Regarding Leading and Deciding, Julie Siwicky, who spent time in India and New Zealand reflects, "I do feel that I learned how to be more decisive and a better leader. I remember traveling with a group of strangers (who would become great friends) in New Zealand. None of us wanted to be the one to make big decisions for the group – where to eat, how to plan out our days, which bus to catch. ... Soon, I had an epiphany: people wanted someone to start making decisions, regardless of what they were. So I started making them, reluctantly at first. By the end of the trip, and really by the end of the gap year, I had developed much more confidence in my leadership skills. I'm still growing and learning them, but that moment sticks out for me as a point when I realized their importance."

Wes Cannon, who worked on ships before returning to school with greater confidence and leadership abilities, says "I became a first mate on tall ships. I was responsible for the safety and running of other people and passengers. This was a big responsibility and gave me lots of confidence in other roles and the ability to assume leadership when necessary."

Andrea Chace Wessling, who participated in the Dynamy program in Massachusetts says, "I think at one point during Outward Bound, our instructors told me that I had leadership potential, that I just had to believe in myself and what I was saying and doing, and that people would respect me. I had never seen this quality in myself, so it was surprising and flattering. I think it helped me step into leadership positions during college and be more vocal."

And Jon Teel, who is living his dream of working abroad that was born during his gap year reflects, "I definitely gained new leadership abilities because of my gap year. I led a group through the dark while in Hawaii hiking as one example. I had to be more independent and to do numerous things on my own." These gappers now see themselves as leaders when they look in the mirror.

Adapting and Coping

In describing the competency of Adapting and Coping, Caroline Ivy, who became a global citizen through serving orphans in South America observes: "A skill I developed was becoming comfortable in almost any situation. When I start a new job or project, I adjust to the people I am with and I can function well. I can be comfortable in situations with people that my peers probably would not be able to adjust to as quickly. The best skill I gained was that I learned how to laugh at myself. I made tons of mistakes, and instead of getting bent out of shape about them, I found the humor. I also found humor in things that other people would not – especially during rough times, I was able to use humor to keep myself going. This is important – you won't get too far in life taking yourself and your life seriously all the time."

Allison Gilbert, who studied and interned in the UK, says that "One major skill I acquired was being able to work with difficult people. The House of Commons of Parliament was trying enough to an eighteen-year old woman, but in addition to this I was a research assistant for a Member of Parliament whose political and social values were drastically different than mine. Surprisingly, it wasn't the differences between our values that made working in his office a challenge. It was the absurd demands and different personalities that I had to confront. I learned how to maintain professionalism, meet the needs of others without compromising my own, and learned that sometimes others can be wrong, even when they insist they are not."

Owen Genzlinger, who confirmed his love of flying and the value of meeting and overcoming challenges during his gap year, offers, "My religious beliefs were tested and made more concrete. I can stand up for what I believe in, and another's person opinion is not going to change that. That doesn't mean that I don't listen to other people. I'm not swayed by everything other people say is all."

Supporting and Cooperating

When it comes to an example of Supporting and Cooperating, Bathsheba Demuth, who wrote a book about her experiences in Old Crow, Yukon states: "Preparing for sled dog races is very much a team effort, and I really enjoyed working with my host family. I had to adjust to living in a different culture very quickly, and ended up making some of the best friends I've ever had while in the Arctic."

Maggie Hureau, who worked for City Year after her two years as a corps member says that, "This is one area in which I think I excelled since my gap year. The program I worked for emphasized the importance of teamwork so when I attended college and in work situations I feel that I was among the few who could truly grasp the concept of teamwork."

David Lofgren, who learned financial and practical independence, and how to serve on a team, told us that "I learned working in the Washington Conservation Corps how to take a back seat. I found that I could anticipate the needs of the group and that of the leader. It became clear to me that not only was I part of the team, but I knew what my role was in the team."

******

As alums grow more self aware, the development of a gap year narrative plays a prominent role in more formal education and job-related contexts. We have alluded to the finding that the experience often becomes an integral part of the college or graduate-professional admissions process, either as part of essays or interviews or both. Many alums saw themselves differently in the college applications they wrote prior to their gap year and those they wrote after. And employers (in the estimate of those we interviewed) often saw the experiences as ones that differentiated gap year alums from other candidates, frequently leading to an interview and opportunity that otherwise might not have been available.

Reflecting, Blogs, and Journals

One of the areas that we explored with the gappers we interviewed was the extent to which they documented their experiences by keeping a journal, sending e-mails, taking pictures, or developing blogs. This question was intended to explore how gappers reflected upon their experience in real time, while they were in the zone of a gap experience. Parents often comment that they saw transformations taking place via the messages that they received (e-mail or letters) or in some cases via blogs that programs or students used to keep others informed of the experience. Many students ask their parents to pass on the emails to family and friends who may be interested in the journey.

Such was the case of Andrew Rosseau, whose participation in a blog helped him come to understand the difference in school-based writing and writing for a broader purpose. Andrew noted that his writing during his gap year was based on what was important to him whereas in school he had to first "figure out the teachers and plug in their quirks in order to get an A." Andrew's mother, Noel, observed that his writing on the Global Learning Across Borders' blog was a new experience because he had a much different set of readers than when he was writing primarily for teachers in school.

As part of our interview we asked all of our gappers: *Was there a specific experience or incident (positive or negative/a challenge) that stands out that helped you discover something about who you are as a person and what you think is important?* David Lofgren was especially thankful to have taken the time to document his experiences for himself in a daily journal. He recounted one particularly stressful situation during his time in France when his backpack was stolen.

He said that his reactions to this loss constituted a memorable journal entry. Reflecting on this incident as a "tipping point" in his gap year experience, David says he had to clarify his values and evaluate how he could move forward after the blow of losing lots of material things at a critical time. He never thought of returning home as an option. He found solace instead in the support of the French villagers and the farm families for whom he was slated to work; or as he put it, he "found out how genuinely kind people can be." David discovered he was resilient – able to bounce back quickly from setbacks and maintain an optimistic outlook by accepting his loss along with the help of strangers.

Cristina Harris was an enthusiastic journalist, making daily entries on her trip to Italy to study art and Italian and on her hiking expedition in Utah. She later found it difficult to read her account of these two periods as it tends to make her too nostalgic. Her memories of her experiences, especially her time backpacking through the desert in Utah, are vivid. In response to our question on skills, knowledge, or abilities gained as a result of her year, she cites the challenge of what is called a solo experience in which she was alone in the desert for twenty-four hours.

During this time, she was inspired to reflect on what music had always meant to her. She soon found herself drawing a keyboard in the sand and she began playing on the makeshift keys. From this experience she drew lessons that are standing her in good stead as she prepares to face obstacles that may present themselves to her as an aspiring female musician. The most important result or outcome of Cristina's experience was that she learned that "there are no limits, just those limits you place on yourself."

******

Cristina's experience alone in the desert on her solo and her conclusion that the only limits are those we place on ourselves illustrates the inspiration that many gappers shared with us that one of their goals for their gap year was to get outside their comfort zones. One of the limits that many Americans tend to place on themselves is a fear of being on one's own and by one's self. Being alone is, by this definition, outside our comfort zones. Leon Botstein, a symphony conductor, president of Bard College, and author of *Jefferson's Children: Education and the Promise of American Culture*, describes an antidote to a concern about being alone: "We fear that our children will be lonely. In general, Americans are terrified of loneliness. But the only effective antidote to loneliness is the ability to spend time alone, to be content and happy by oneself. ... The capacity to relish spending time alone, doing something with a sense of accomplishment by oneself, and experiencing for oneself, is an important survival skill."

One reason many gappers choose to travel is a desire to be on their own and, as a result, become more comfortable with being alone. Adam, our gapper son, noted that this was a highlight of his gap year and one effective way to get to know himself.

Traveling alone abroad can be an immensely powerful tool for developing confidence and 'road warrior' status. I traveled alone in Costa Rica for a month or so after my two structured programs in New Zealand and Central America. After having been supervised for six months (not to mention the eighteen years I spent at home), I felt the need to strike out on my own a little bit more, this time, alone. Being solitary in a foreign country is in a category all by itself in my opinion because you become, at some point along the way, your only friend. This is a point when introspection becomes a pastime and learning about your self is a daily if not an hourly occurrence.

Chelsea Rogers also discovered value in being alone. "Seeing new things puts a different perspective on your own life. Traveling alone in a new place forced me to become more self-confident and outgoing." Chelsea's experiences included time in Archelon in Greece helping preserve sea turtles and at a language school in Italy. She says that the work "with children in poverty stricken villages in Costa Rica was probably the most rewarding experience of my life and taught me a lot about life."

Erin O'Neil found she was more reflective and valued time alone during her gap year. "I was very, very introspective. When I felt uneasy, I would sit alone in a tree, on the beach, or some other beautiful place and just take everything in. The beauty made me relax and realize what an amazing opportunity was in front of me." One way she has tried to capture her experiences is by collecting remembrances. "I have a 'happy box' where I placed paper menus, airline tickets, bus tickets, brochures, mementos, etc. from my trip. I wish I had kept more of a journal, as mine was more introspective and sporadic, but this happy box captures so many memories and details I wouldn't have written about. I would recommend it to anyone."

Malaka Refai reinforces the message that an essential part of a gap year experience is learning to travel on one's own, using the opportunity to learn more about "this person named Malaka... because I was the only certainty I had."

Louis Lobel discovered the power of being on his own and reflecting during his time teaching in India.

> I got to create my own path and go wherever I want. I think one of the main ways I benefited was learning to be alone which is an extremely important thing because while as a high-schooler you can feel isolated, lonely, like no one understands you. You always have some type of supervision, and college is really liberating because it's like the school atmosphere without the parents. You get to go crazy. Which is why a lot of people freshman year go too crazy almost. So a semester off made me confront myself for the first time ever because I've always had someone else to interact with. I've never actually had to face myself and who I was and who I wanted to be and what direction I wanted to go in my life.

******

The research literature on young adult development helps to frame these reflections in substantive terms. In *Finding Flow: The Psychology of Engagement with Everyday Life*, Mihaly Csikszentmihalyi, who is professor of psychology Claremont Graduate University in California, comments on the importance of friendships in life. He then notes the importance of what appears to be a gap year-related skill.

> The strong effects of companionship on the quality of experience suggest that investing psychic energy in relationships is a good way to improve life. ... But for real

growth it is necessary to find people whose opinions are interesting and whose conversation is stimulating. A more difficult, but in the long run even more useful, skill to acquire is the ability to tolerate solitude and even enjoy it.

Ben Ewing's adventures in Peru helped him to understand the importance of getting outside your comfort zone as an integral part of life preparation. He found that he had to learn Spanish quickly as a matter of gaining a foothold socially in a new culture. He also had to develop other skills to fend for himself in making arrangements during his travels.

> If you're not put in new situations, then how are you going to prepare yourself for a really huge new situation? So put yourself in any kind of new experience, any kind of situation where you have to fend for yourself. Situations where you have to be independent and do things that you're not used to doing by yourself, whether that's speaking a different language or making money for yourself, or being in a new place where usually your parents would be the ones finding the hotel, finding the food, finding the transportation. Just doing that by yourself, that alone can build up that kind of independence, an experience you can build on later, and you can use for college.

Parents Look In the Mirror

Gap years are opportunities for parents to grow as well and to take a good look in the mirror, to examine the extent to which their fears can impose limits on their child's ability (in Leon Botstein's words) to "cultivate their own distinct personalities...to think for themselves, and stand up for themselves." In a family's assessment of any major decision, such as seriously considering a gap year, a parent's protective instincts can be a barrier, as we saw in the survey. We asked our alums to rate different barriers to their considering gap years on a scale of one to ten, with ten being the highest rating. The top two answers, equally ranked, are the concerns of parents or guardians and lack of information about gap year alternatives.

Other parents take the lead in suggesting a gap year option to their son or daughter. Daniel Krass, Becca Krass's dad, initiated the conversation about not going directly to college. He reflected on the importance of the parental role as the source of gap year information, if not inspiration, when he said that he believes: "No kid hears about gap years on their own. The concept has to come from the parent as a positive alternative or option." Other parents, such as Amy Ivy, specifically mentioned her desire to refrain from being a "helicopter parent." She did not see her role as being the responsible one for the choice of gap year programs or being the ever-ready intervener when problems arose.

Stories in the press now detail the impact that exceptionally involved parenting has on children's experiences from summer camp to college applications and even job interviews and salary negotiations. The gap year parents we met offer hope that these overly-protective parenting styles may grow to be exceptions. Gap year experiences also appear to have positive impacts on the relationships that alums develop with their parents, with each encouraging the other not to take the counsel of their fears. And to trust in the fact, as gap alums as well as developmental psychologists remind us, that solitude and leaving the nest to grow away from home are not necessarily bad things. As parents see their kids as their reflections, we might learn to trust that they, too, can continue to grow and mature.

A reminder of what such a willingness on the part of parents can mean are the words of gap alum Leigh James, who backpacked in Hawaii and sailed around Australia as part of her gap year. She commented on the contribution of her year and of her parents to her development. "After college I lived and worked abroad for two years. There is no way I would have ever had the courage to do this if I hadn't traveled during my gap year. I would say the gap year helped me eliminate fear in where I lived and what I'm capable of doing. I think courage was one of the biggest gifts I received from the gap year."

The observations of gappers we interviewed and their parents have led us to conclude that there is something powerful about gap years in helping young adults to develop a better understanding of themselves. When you hear parents speak of the opportunity for their son or daughter to discover him or herself, to develop self-confidence and learn to be in the moment, it becomes clear that there is more occurring than time passing. Becoming more "mature" means actively seeing oneself in terms of a life story, adding richness to life through experiences, learning through service to others, developing uncommon friendships, and seeing (and being seen) by your family in new ways.

Gappers express the growth they experience in many ways, but it begins with self-knowledge that they can articulate and that their parents can witness in their actions. In the words of a gap parent, Libba Williams, speaking of the impact of her son Harris's year, "He has an air of independence and self-confidence, a 'can-do' attitude and, most importantly, he is happy with himself."

The Journey as Narrative

Based on quantitative survey answers and qualitative reflections, we can offer that a gap journey may help young men and women understand themselves better. Jonathan Haidt, associate professor of psychology at the University of Virginia, cites research in his book, *The Happiness Hypothesis*, that informs the journey of self-discovery in terms of seminal studies in the levels of personality. He references work done by psychologists on the way in which, at the highest level of functioning, one goes about translating experience into self-understanding.

> You create your story in consciousness as you interpret your own behavior, and as you listen to other people's thoughts about you. The life story is not the work of a historian... it is more like a work of historical fiction that makes plenty of references to real events and connects them by dramatizations and interpretations that might or might not be true to the spirit of what happened.

Pierce Delahunt developed a keen awareness of what gap year experiences can mean to a life narrative. His extensive travels through the U.S., Mexico, and Canada included trips, mostly on a Greyhound bus, to visit friends at a variety of college campuses. He also attended Tom Brown's Tracker School in New Jersey, learned dog-sledding in Minnesota, served as an apprentice to an artist in Mexico, and studied blade-smithing in Arkansas. He traveled to Europe and Brazil, in the latter case, working at a jaguar preserve in the spring and summer as part of his gap year.

When asked whether he discovered something about himself during his gap year, Pierce said that "Your interactions with others define the self and you discover yourself in the doing, defining who you are by experience." His interactions with people around the world convinced him that one should never underestimate the scope of the human personality. In talking with others about his time, Pierce began to construct a story, a self-conscious gap year narrative that people could relate to easily. His experience of telling his story helped him realize the importance of putting things into words, including in his Facebook entries. He says that through his nonfiction storytelling he sought to inspire others with the challenge, "Isn't life great?"

The narrative that gappers like Pierce can develop is one that they share with those closest to them when they return from a journey. As we found in response to the survey question, *After you returned from your gap year experience (in the first year back), how frequently did you find that you discussed what you learned or discovered with friends or family?*, 67 percent of gappers reported that they spoke of their experience very frequently (once per week) and another 27 percent reported that they spoke frequently of their experience (once a month). We also learned that often times these accounts fell on deaf ears because the audience of friends or family could not seem to appreciate the full significance of the experience. This perceived lack of understanding led those like gap alum Julia Bloch to wonder, "How can you say you love me but you can't understand?"

From the survey data we conclude that gappers continue to share their stories as gap year promoters long after the specific journey ends. In response to the survey question, *Which of the following roles would you say best describes your advocacy of gap years?*, 84 percent said they recommended or spoke frequently to others about gap years.

Eris Dyson

The power of gap year experiences, their poignancy for gappers, and their practical impact in real life contexts, is exemplified by Eris Dyson, a City Year volunteer from Cleveland, Ohio. Eris Dyson is a student, author, poet, and leader who credits City Year with changing her life. When we spoke, she was attending Notre Dame College, a private school in Cleveland, Ohio. Notre Dame's Dean of Admissions had met with her City Year group. He was so impressed by the corps members' attitudes, leadership abilities, and teamwork skills that he offered fifty percent off of tuition for alums who chose to attend Notre Dame. "I always wanted to go to college, but City Year made it possible," Eris says. The Notre Dame Dean was not the only one impressed by City Year corps members. Eris notes that the regional CVS drug store executive saw the members had leadership and organizational competencies his company needed. He set up a program to recruit City Year graduates straight into a management training program.

At Notre Dame, Eris is majoring in public relations, a choice she made based on her experience at City Year. "I learned how to plan events and write press releases. I learned how to be a very good speaker and a very good writer, by doing the work that had to be done. That's why I'm a public relations major." Eris is planning on going to graduate school to earn a degree in non-profit management and social work, dedicated to using her "power and talents for good, not for evil."

You can't talk with Eris without being struck by her passion for poetry, serving, and for helping others. Her voice changes when she talks about a fourteen-year old Eris who was searching to find herself and who was impressed by City Year members she met during a volunteer activity. We asked what fourteen-year old Eris would think of herself today.

Eris at fourteen could barely look in the mirror and think she was beautiful, smart, or had any worth. Eris at fourteen felt isolated and alone. The only way that I found myself was through doing community service and poetry. It saved my life. Sometimes working with kids, it's difficult not to take problems home with you. You see them wearing the same shirt for two weeks. You know that the meal at school is their only real meal during the day. You wonder what they'll have to eat on weekends.

Eris spent her early years growing up in inner-city Cleveland and can relate to the challenges facing the students she served.

For those kids, you're their glimmer of hope. They will never, ever forget you. Never, ever. It makes you hold yourself accountable. You work hard to be a better person, because they're watching you. I have to work hard to be the best person I can be because I'm an example to them. Hopefully, they will be able to make a difference. I tell them they need to grow up to be role models for my children and other children.

Eris says she's still thinking about herself at age fourteen. "I would tell fourteen-year-old Eris, 'Don't worry. It won't always be easy. You're going to be hurt, you're going to cry. But it will make you be able to relate to others. You will be okay. You will develop the power and ability to be able to go and use those words – your poetry – in community service and make it even more powerful.'"

"I'll never have a nine-to-five job," she states confidently. "I'll help students and youth. I'll be a role model." And whatever she does will include poetry, service, and combine the City Year ethic.

Eris's life narrative, her story, and her understanding of herself as a role model for others in her community demonstrate the potential to translate a gap year experience into a legacy. The influences of a gap year can extend beyond what gappers see in the mirror. The impacts can ripple in the social circles of family and friends and extend into relationships at work, in school, and beyond our borders.

******

Although a gap year is not an option for everybody, we hope that these stories of self-discovery will inspire more to recognize there is a beneficial alternative to going straight to college. Gapper Julia Bloch's advice for those thinking about this option is: "Go. Do. Be." In the words of one parent who was asked her advice for other parents considering their role in the journey, "Give them the wings and let them fly."

Gap Year Survey Findings Summary

- *What do gap alums believe was the most important outcome of their experience?* The top answer in the survey was that it "gave them a better sense of who they are as a person."

- *After returning from a gap year experience (in the first year back), how frequently do gappers discuss what they learned or discovered with friends or family?* Sixty-seven percent in the survey reported that they spoke of their experiences very frequently (once per week) and another 27 percent reported that they spoke of their experiences frequently (once a month).

- *How do gap alums express their advocacy of gap years?* The top answer (84 percent) was that they recommended or spoke frequently to others about gap years.

- *How do gappers recognize self growth (even if not consciously at first)?* They report that spending time alone can lead to reflection and self-awareness. They also report that blogs, emails, journals, and other forms of documentation help them process experiences. When they look back on the documentation, they can see evidence of self-growth.

Tips

- *Growth through giving.* A primary source of growth during a gap year is giving to others. As gap students talk about their time off, listen for evidence of their self-awareness even if they are talking about external experiences.

- *Choices about free time.* An indicator of self awareness for many gappers may be how they choose to spend free time after a gap year compared to before. For example, a young person who previously watched TV and went to the mall may invest more free time reading and reflecting – as one alum put it, "spending time doing what I am interested in as opposed to what others want me to do."

- *Hang onto emails, blogs, journals, etc.* Gappers and their parents may want to hold on to reflective and descriptive documentation produced during a gap year, even for years to come. They can be valuable reminders and resilience-boosters over time.

- For gappers: "Go. Do. Be."

- For parents/guardians: "Give them the wings and let them fly."

Chapter Nine

CONTINUING THE JOURNEY

The journey began with a practical definition of a gap year: "a gap year or gap experience is a time when a young person takes a structured break before high school or during college." In trying to further define the impact of gap years for young adults in America, we've listened carefully to the voices of those who have taken the journey themselves. What they have shared leads to provisional conclusions on the impact of their experiences and a way to begin to define gap years, American style.

In the previous chapters, we offered findings on the impact of gap years in areas of education, finance, careers, service, and global citizenship. In the area of education, a provisional finding is that gap years can lead to a reinvigorated interest in education and learning, and to students' being actively involved and even sensing "ownership" of their education. In the area of finance, our research shows that gap years can be less expensive than college and can even result in gappers earning money toward college. Young adults who have taken a break report being both more financially aware and more conscious of the contrast between wealth and poverty on a global scale.

For the workplace, gappers report developing valuable skills during their experiences – whether in the United States or the United

Kingdom. With economic challenges leading more students to delay college, there has been an increased interest in gap year options that can help pay for school such as internships. During these experiences, students develop skills that are valued by employers and may give gap alums a leg up on the competition when applying for jobs. In the UK, employers actively recruit gap year students. It is not insignificant in this regard that gap alums also report being more satisfied in their careers than others of their generation.

When it comes to volunteering, young adults who have chosen to help others through gap experiences value the "opportunity to serve others" as a primary benefit of their time away from formal education. In their careers, most gappers (even those who didn't volunteer in a programmatic sense) seem to embrace the opportunity to gain new skills and internalize a service ethic to a higher degree than their peers. Most gappers, those who've gone abroad and those who have stayed in the United States, say they have gained greater appreciation and a greater understanding of other people, cultures, and religions. They can view themselves as more globally aware, compared to their peers, upon their return to college.

Given these impacts in defined areas, it is reasonable to conclude that gap years provide practical competitive advantages in the areas of education, finance, and the workplace. A provisional conclusion also is that gap years can lead to what some view as higher-order values that we try to encourage in young people and all citizens the United States. These may include incorporating a serving ethic and seeing oneself as more globally and culturally aware.

Revisiting our original definition of a gap year – as taking a structured break before or during college – we propose to add a fragment on the impacts of gap years to distinguish "gap year, American style." Here's a tentative re-wording: "A gap year, American style, is an individual journey taken before or during college, that can result in positive impacts for an individual in areas of self-awareness, education, finance, career, and the ability to serve others."

We've heard an emphasis on the *individual* nature of American gap year experiences as distinguished from more of a collective mentality in other countries. They are characterized by a journey of self-discovery that is continuously reinforced by a commitment to life-long learning and serving.

Defined in this way, the interest in gap years from a variety of potential stakeholders may broaden in the years to come as it already has in other countries. The interested parties may include educators, employers, and public policy decision-makers.

******

As government officials and private citizens, we have contributed over the years to the development of public policy recommendations, particularly in the areas of education and workforce development. There are numerous associations, not-for-profit organizations, lobbying and government groups vocal in policy arenas that are dedicated to the development of young people in America and around the world. We believe that gap years deserve a voice at the policy table and welcome the opportunity for the dialogue. In the spirit of the gappers who have shared their stories, however, we offer broad observations and suggestions for those interested in joining or continuing the journey rather than specific policy recommendations.

High School Counselors and Educators

For high school counselors and educators, this could mean becoming more conversant with gap year alternatives and actively listening for individual students and their parents who might be candidates for such an option. Consider inviting gap alums or their parents who want to share their stories with other students into schools and classrooms, or consider hosting an evening forum on the topic. Schools might consider supporting educators interested in accompanying students to experience a gap journey first-hand, encouraging teachers to integrate "lessons learned" into school activities and curricula.

Colleges and Universities

For college and university officials, a focus on gap years could mean examining practices and policies to determine where their institutions fall on a spectrum of acceptance of the concept.

- Do they recognize gap years as an option in policy statements?
- Do they suggest that students can consider gap years as an option in acceptance letters?
- Do they grant deferrals?
- Are officials aware of resources where students, parents, and educators can go to learn more about gap year issues and options?
- Do they offer credit for gap year experiences?
- Do they have programs, grants, or scholarships that support gap students?
- Does the campus community recognize the individual gap year journey and provide an in-person or on-line venue for students to share their experiences?
- Is there support for gap students who arrive at, or return to, campus?

Gap Year Program Providers and Consultants

Program providers and consultants are obviously key, valued, and valuable stakeholders in advancing gap years. They might consider how gap years fit into the broader picture of education options for all students as they make the case. They might look for ways to ensure that gap years in America retain the flexibility that encourages and respects individuality, while ensuring a high quality of standards regarding all aspects of a young adult's experience. (The American Gap Association's accreditation process is a milestone in the direction of quality standards.) Programs could consider integrating competencies into the structure or curriculum so that all students have the opportunity to develop skills that will help them succeed in college, in the workplace, and in life. Individually or collectively, they might seek to manage commercialization that is likely to perpetuate if the predictions about an American gap year growth market are true.

Program providers could allow and even encourage an entrepreneurial gap year spirit for newcomers and even risk-takers in program development. Perhaps they could consider partnering to expand or initiate opportunities that continue to open doors for young adults from all socioeconomic backgrounds to participate, including expanding scholarships and grants. They may also offer advice on practical and creative ways to pay for gap year experiences (as many already do!). And programs might look to build on efforts to effectively gauge the impact of programs on participants, months and even years after gappers have left the structured aspects of a program.

Researchers

For researchers (including foundations who support research), we hope there will be continuing efforts to document the impact of gap years – positive and negative. These areas might include:

- conducting international and work-based research (using, for example, SHL's Great Eight competency model);
- assessing individuals, groups, or program participants against the gapper benchmarks in the survey used for this research;
- considering the impact of gap experiences on family relationships and bonds before, during, and after the gap year journey; and
- continuing to research the impacts on education, careers, financial awareness, service, and self-discovery.

Government

For government, as a first step, there may be an opportunity to recognize gap years as an educational option. For the U.S. Department of Education, this could mean defining gap years more precisely in longitudinal data – rather than lumping gappers in with others who don't immediately go onto college. The U.S. Department of Labor might consider pilot studies on the relevance of skills developed during gap years and employability, possibly in partnership with the U.S. Department of Education. The U.S. Department of State might continue to review policies that encourage and discourage international gap experiences – for American students going abroad, and for international students who choose the United States as a gap destination. The U.S. Department of Defense might consider a program like that of

Australia's in which gap year candidates spend a year in the nation's military and "try out" military careers as an option upon high school graduation, with no commitment to sign up for service.

State governments and local school districts also might assess their awareness of gap years as an alternative to a more traditional path through school, especially as we look for policies and programs that make the learning experiences of young people ages 16-18 richer and more meaningful. The expansion of AmeriCorps (as well as programs such as Year Up and Dynamy's Youth Academy) represent advancements in opening up gap opportunities for a wider spectrum of candidates. Government at all levels might consider the internships and opportunities it has in place as gap year options and how to better connect with parents, students, and educators about their availability.

Employers

Employers might begin to recognize that young people with real-world experience could help fill the "gap" they are experiencing in finding employees with the skills and attitudes needed to succeed in the local economy and global marketplace. They could consider internship opportunities that fit into a gap itinerary, and ways to evaluate and recognize skills-related performance. They might even take a lead from counterparts in the UK and Ireland in developing gap year scholarships and opportunities or recognizing the value of a gap year as a complement to formal education.

Students and Parents

There are two groups that we did not include in the list of potential gap year stakeholders above. For them, we offer a final thought. If students and parents are reading the stories and results offered in this book, we hope you believe there is at least a case to be made that a gap alternative to the traditional education track is worthy of consideration, maybe for you or for someone you know.

Through the eyes of young adults who happen to have had gap experiences, we have come to see the gap year concept as characterized by their confidence, curiosity, an openness to learning from others, learning while doing and serving, and learning about oneself along the way. They ask questions in terms of others to explore, always listen to answers, and at least try to understand what appears foreign – outside their comfort zone. A good question for parents and students to ask, then, may not be "When do gappers return to the classroom and get back on track?" but to ask what they continue to learn upon their return that will enrich their lives and rival what they have learned on their respective journeys.

Shanna Silverberg, one of our gap alums, noted that after her experience "the American Dream doesn't seem to connect with the world we live in." Others we have talked with agree that the traditional sense of an American Dream, as those on the treadmill and potentially prone to status anxiety would define it, seems foreign to them. What they can connect with is a new aspect to a Global Dream characterized by a journey of self-discovery that is continuously reinforced by a commitment to life-long learning and serving. This notion may bring us back to considering the greatness of youthful aspiration such as that found in those who saw themselves establishing a *novus ordo saeclorum* – a "new order of the ages." We may ask ourselves how, in proposing to open the door to new experiences , we might see ourselves, our sons, and our daughters in their image.

Such could become the ethic of a fulfilling life, the promise and example that the young people found here and elsewhere can hold up for each of us and to the world – as they choose to define it.

We are confident that the journey continues for the young men and women profiled in this book, each on a uniquely individual path. And we hope these wanderers would be provisionally content with the notion that gap years, American style, can also be defined as a pivotal part of an individual's journey toward learning, serving, and self-discovery.

Appendix

GAP YEAR PARTNERS

This book would not have been possible without the partners referenced below. The program partners, consulting partners, and experts have excellent resources for more information about gap year options. The advertising firm of Horward Merrell & Partners, and SHL – the global leader in workforce assessment and talent analytics – have provided invaluable expertise and support as our principal private sector partners. *Please check websites for updated information.*

Programs, Consulting Partners, and Experts

Center for Interim Programs, LLC

The Center for Interim Programs is a consulting service that helps young people find meaningful gap year placements. Since its inception in 1980 as the first organization of its kind in the United States, Interim has designed creative gap year opportunities for more than 5,000 young people. Interim has built relationships with organizations worldwide and offers a database of more than 5,200 program opportunities. Interim works one-on-one with clients to identify programs that match their interests, needs, and goals. Interim guides clients through the process of identifying opportune gap year programs, securing placements and outlining ways to make the most of this unique opportunity.

Contact Information:

Website: www.interimprograms.com
Email: info@interimprograms.com

New Jersey Office:
195 Nassau Street, 2nd Floor, Suite #5
Princeton, NJ 08542
Phone: 609-683-4300

Massachusetts Office:
6 Center Street, Suite 318
Northampton, MA 01060
Phone: 413-585-0980

******

City Year, Inc.

In 1988, City Year was founded by Michael Brown and Alan Khazei, then-roommates at Harvard Law School, who felt strongly that young people in service could be a powerful resource for addressing our nation's most pressing issues. City Year supports this goal through its signature program, a Full Time Youth Service Corps, among other initiatives. Each year, it unites more than 1,400 young people ages seventeen to twenty-four for a demanding year of full-time community service, leadership development, and civic engagement. Participants come from diverse backgrounds and serve by tutoring and mentoring in schools, reclaiming public spaces, and organizing after-school programs and school vacation camps, among other programs.

Contact Information:

Website: www.cityyear.org

City Year Headquarters:
287 Columbus Avenue
Boston, MA 02116
Phone: 617-927-2500

******

Collegeology

There are many doors students can open after high school. The Collegeology team explores options with students and helps guide them through the door of their dreams. Collegeology has had years of experience helping students who choose to take a less traditional path to college, such as a gap year. Some of the options Collegeology points to include: post-graduate study abroad; organized travel experiences; volunteer experiences within the U.S. and abroad; and career internships.

Contact Information:

Website: www.collegeology.com
Email: through website form

927 North Northlake Way, Suite 300
Seattle, WA 98103
Phone: 206-633-0443

******

Dynamy

Dynamy, Inc., is a not-for-profit experiential educational organization founded in 1969. It is the oldest and only residential internship program in the country. Its mission is to offer young people, ages seventeen to twenty-two, a gap year opportunity like no other. Dynamy believes that the prerequisites for work- and life-readiness are independence, self-reliance, courage, character, a habit of service, and an ability to build healthy relationships. It believes that these things can be learned best through experience. Dynamy programs integrate independent city apartment living with mentored internships, personal and college/career advising, urban and wilderness leadership opportunities, and the company of an incredible group of peers. By arranging internship programs that involve valuable mentoring, leadership training, and outdoor challenges, Dynamy helps young people increase their competence, confidence, and sense of connection to society.

Contact information:

Website: www.dynamy.org
Email: info-email@dynamy.org

Administrative office:
27 Sever Street
Worcester, MA
Phone: 508-755-2571

******

LEAPNOW

Founded in 1994, LEAPNOW provides students with access to thousands of diverse international and domestic learning experiences in 126 countries, and offers transformational teachings that give students the opportunity to empower themselves to "*be the change that you wish to see in the world*" (Gandhi). Cultural immersion, study abroad, and work abroad are the main vehicles for participants' learning about themselves and the world. Intense work and study experiences abroad are complemented with contemplative learning retreats at the northern California campus that serve to teach students how to wholeheartedly participate in the world and live passionately without leaving any parts of themselves out – mind, body, spirit, soul, emotion, etc.

Contact information:

Website: www.leapnow.org
Email: info@leapnow.org

11640 Highway 128
Calistoga, CA 94515
Phone: 888-424-5327

******

Pioneer Project

The Pioneer Project's motto is "exploring inner frontiers." It offers semester and year-long gap year programs focused on homesteading, crafts, and wilderness expeditions in the Appalachian Mountains. Its mission is "to foster clarity of purpose, empowerment, and interdependence in young adults by offering a community-oriented educational experience." Through "getting their hands in the dirt," Pioneer Project students "rejoice in the power of learning through experience, not textbooks. After being exposed to a diverse suite of experiences, they begin to hone in on what they are passionate about and what they will pursue on their path to co-creating a better world. Students become true pioneers who not only possess the intrinsic confidence that sprouts from self-reliance, but also embark on the risky journey of 'following their bliss.'"

Contact information:

Website: www.pioneerproject.org
Email: info@pioneerproject.org

479 Pine Log Church Road
Brasstown, NC 28902
Phone: 336-324-3917

******

Student Extended Experiences Consulting, Inc.

Marsha Ray is founder and director of Student Extended Experiences Consulting, Inc. (SEEC, Inc.) which helps students create and design dynamic gap years of sabbatical experiences. As a long-time educator in U.S., French, and Italian high schools and with years of teaching at DePaul University in Chicago, Marsha Ray helps American students understand the value of the international experience. She is located near Chicago and has served students from all over the U.S. for more than fifteen years.

Contact information:

Website: www.seectimeout.com
Email: seecray@sbcglobal.net
Phone: 847-374-0791

******

Dr. Monica Andrews

Dr. Monica Andrews is an educational expert who has interviewed families both before and after the students' gap experiences, as well as other experts on the topic. Her research on the gap year grew out of more general research begun in 2005 on how high school students choose colleges, apply to colleges, transition into colleges, and complete college. Dr. Andrews has been teaching research methods and writing since 1987, first as a teaching fellow at Harvard, then at University of California (Santa Barbara) as well as Endicott College. She has created a DVD to guide families in the process of planning a meaningful and productive gap year. The DVD can be previewed and purchased at www.ReelWisdom.com.

Contact Information:

www.ReelWisdom.com

******

Survey and Research Partners

Howard, Merrell & Partners

Raleigh, NC-based Howard, Merrell & Partners, Inc., specializes in linking business and communications strategies to yield higher levels of financial performance for its clients. The agency is a pioneer in understanding and applying the power of emotions to develop more effective business and communications strategies. Agency service offerings include brand development, creative development and production, consumer insight research, public relations, media asset services, event planning, and management and strategic account management.

Contact Information:

Website: www.merrellgroup.com
Email: info@merrellgroup.com

8521 Six Forks Road, Suite 400
Raleigh, N.C. 27615
Phone: 919-848-2400

******

SHL Group Ltd.

SHL was founded in the UK in 1977 by Peter Saville and Roger Holdsworth. In the early 90's SHL began to establish offices internationally and now has offices in 40 countries, in the Asia Pacific region, in the Americas, South Africa, and Europe. It is a world leader of objective assessment for the workplace. The firm was uniquely able to facilitate secondary analysis of UK research on gap years and employment that allowed comparison with the U.S. gap year research.

Contact Information:

Website: www.shl.com/us

Atlanta Office:
555 North Point Center East
Floor 6
Alpharetta, GA 30022
Phone: 770.650.8080

GAP YEAR
BIBLIOGRAPHY

Adelman, Clifford. 2006. *The Toolbox Revisited: Paths to Degree Completion from High School through College*. Washington: U.S. Department of Education.

Aristotle. 1990. *Nicomachean Ethics in Great Books of the Western World*. Trans. W.D. Ross. Chicago: Encyclopedia Britannica.

Arnett, Jeffrey. 2004. *Emerging Adulthood: The Winding Road from the Late Teens through the Twenties*. New York: Oxford University Press.

Bien, Peter. 2000. "Odysseus Across the Centuries." Lecture to The Society for the Preservation of the Greek Heritage, Washington, D.C., September 18, 2000.

Botstein, Leon. 1997. *Jefferson's Children: Education and the Promise of American Culture*. New York: Doubleday.

Brann, Eva. "The Poet of the Odyssey." 1997. In Pamela Kraus, ed., *The Past-Present: Selected Writings of Eva Brann*, 3-19. Annapolis: St. John's College Press.
   ---. "Benign Interruptions in Students' Progress toward Graduation and Postgraduate Education," *The Placement Office Newsletter*, St. John's College, Santa Fe, NM, 1995.

Brown, Donald. 1991. *Human Universals*. Boston: McGraw-Hill.

Bywater, James, and Jo Wilson. 2006. "The Haystack Is Getting Bigger But Should the Needles Necessarily Be Harder to Find?" *SHL Whitepaper 2006*. London: SHL Group plc.

Cavafy, Constantine. 1992. "Ithaka." Trans. by Edmund Keeley and Philip Sherrard. In George Savidis, ed., *Collected Poems*, Revised Edition. Princeton University Press, 1992.

Clydesdale, Tim. 2007. *The First Year Out: Understanding American Teens after High School*. Chicago: University of Chicago Press.

Cohen, Don and Laurence Prusak. 2001. *In Good Company: How Social Capital Makes Organizations Work*. Boston: Harvard Business School Press.

Creswell, John. 2003. *Research Design: Qualitative, Quantitative and Mixed Methods Approaches*, Second Edition. Thousand Oaks, CA: Sage Publications.

Csikszentmihalyi, Mihaly. 1997. *Finding Flow: The Psychology of Engagement in Everyday Life*. New York: Basic Books.

Csikszentmihalyi, Mihaly and Barbara Schneider, editors. 2000. *Becoming Adult: How Teenagers Prepare for the World of Work*. New York: Basic Books

De Tocqueville, Alexis. 2000. *Democracy in America*. Trans., ed., Harvey Mansfield and Delba Winthrop. Chicago: University of Chicago Press.

Ferry, Luc. 2005. *What Is the Good Life?* Chicago: University of Chicago Press.

Fredrickson, Barbara. 2006. "Nice to know you: Positive emotions, self-other overlap and complex understanding in the formation of a new relationship." *Journal of Positive Psychology* 1(2): 93-106.

Foster, Chad. 1995. *Teenagers: Preparing for the Real World: The Inside Scoop on What You Won't Learn in School.* Duluth, GA: Rising Books.

Gilpin, Robert, and Caroline Fitzgibbons. 1992. *Time Out: Taking a Break from School to Travel, Work, & Study in the U.S. and Abroad.* New York: Simon and Schuster.

Goodman, Steven, and Andrea Leiman. 2007. *College Admissions Together: It Takes a Family.* Sterling, VA: Capital Books.

Graham, Carol Madison. 2011. *Coping with Anti-Americanism: A Guide to Getting the Most Out of Studying Abroad.* Dulles, VA: Potomac Books Inc.

Gray, Kenneth. 2000. *Getting Real: Helping Teens Find Their Future.* Thousand Oaks, CA: Corwin Press.

Griffith, Susan. 2003. *Taking a Gap Year:* 3rd Edition. Oxford: Globe Pequot Press.

Haidt, Jonathan. 2006. *The Happiness Hypothesis: Finding Modern Truth in Ancient Wisdom.* New York: Basic Books.

Haigler, Karl, and Rae Nelson. 2005. *The Gap-Year Advantage: Helping Your Child Benefit from Taking Time Off Before or During College.* New York: St. Martin's Press.

Hall, Colin, and Ron Lieber. 2003. *Taking Time Off: Inspiring Stories of Students Who Enjoyed Successful Breaks from College and How You Can Plan Your Own.* New York: The Princeton Review.

Hindle, Charlotte, Et Al. 2003. *The Gap Year Book: The Definitive Guide to Planning and Taking a Year Out.* United Kingdom: Lonely Planet Publications.

Hobsons Student Intelligence Report. 2006. London: Trendence and Hobsons' Planning and Research Division.

Hugo, Beverly. 1999. *Women & Thru-Hiking on the Appalachian Trail.* Harpers Ferry: Appalachian Trail Conference.

Johnson, Helen, and Christine Schelhas-Miller. 2000. *Don't Tell Me What to Do, Just Send Money: The Essential Parenting Guide for the College Years.* New York: St. Martin's Press.

Kamenetz, Anya. 2006. *Generation Debt: Why Now Is a Terrible Time to Be Young.* New York: Riverhead Books.

Kastner, Laura, and Jennifer Wyatt. 2002. *The Launching Years: Strategies for Parenting from Senior Year to College Life.* New York: Three Rivers Press.

Katchadourian, Herant, and John Boli. 1994. *Cream of the Crop: The Impact of Elite Education in the Decade After College.* New York: Basic Books.

Lakoff, George, and Mark Johnson. 1980. *Metaphors We Live By*. Chicago: University of Chicago Press.

Levine, Madeline. 2006. *The Price of Privilege: How Parental Pressure and Material Advantage Are Creating a Generation of Disconnected and Unhappy Kids*. New York: Harper Collins.

Montiglio, Silvia. 2005. *Wandering in Ancient Greek Culture*. Chicago: University of Chicago Press.

Nussbaum, Martha. 1997. *Cultivating Humanity: A Classical Defense of Reform in Liberal Education*. Cambridge: Harvard University Press.
   ---. 2006. *Frontiers of Justice: Disability, Nationality, Species Membership*. Cambridge: Harvard University Press.

Patching, James. 2007. "SHL Results of GAP Students." Private Correspondence, Hobsons *Student Intelligence Report 2006*. Berlin: Trendence.

Platt, Michael. 1999. "The Young, the Good, and the West." In Ralph C. Hancock, ed., *America, the West, and Liberal Education*. 83-143. New York: Rowman and Littlefield.

Pope, Denise. 2001. *Doing School: How We Are Creating a Generation of Stressed Out, Materialistic and Miseducated Students*. New Haven: Yale University Press.

Spinosa, Charles, and Fernando Flores, Hubert Dreyfus. 1997. *Disclosing New Worlds: Entrepreneurship, Democratic Action, and the Cultivation of Solidarity*. Cambridge: MIT Press.

Thacker, Lloyd, Editor. 2004. *College Unranked: Ending the College Admissions Frenzy*. Cambridge: Harvard University Press.

Van Holthoon, Frits, and David Olson, Editors. 1987. *Common Sense: The Foundations of Social Science*. Lanham, MD: University Press of America.

Wood, Danielle. 2000. *The Uncollege Alternative: Your Guide to Incredible Careers and Amazing Adventures Outside College*. New York: Harper Collins.

ACKNOWLEDGMENTS

Thank you, first and foremost, to the gap year alumni and the parents who shared their stories. Many of their names are included in the pages of this book. For all, may your journey continue and may we meet again along the way.

Thank you to Holly Bull for expertise, inspiration, and friendship based on her own interim experience and those of the thousands of students she's guided since. We are grateful to Holly, Joanna Lazarek, and Kate Warren for their interest and patience throughout the process. We are grateful to Mimi Bull, who as a gap year mother and supporter of her husband, Neil, shared stories about the early years of the Center for Interim Programs, LLC.

We are indebted to the firm of Howard, Merrill & Partners for providing the professional and technical expertise that made the quantitative research possible. Dr. Bruce Hall and Rett Haigler provided invaluable assistance. We will always remember and benefit from the wise counsel of Bruce (also a gapper) to "make enough of the data, but not too much."

Sean McDevitt at City Year Inc., as an early supporter, encouraged corps members to participate in the survey, and provided important feedback on the City Year service ethic.

Greg Cappello, formerly of Dynamy, also was instrumental in encouraging young adults to participate in the survey. Fred Kaelin, also of Dynamy, shared insight and stories, including about what can happen when young adults are able to successfully confront their fears.

Marsha Ray was an inspiration as a gap year parent and college advisor, and helped widen the connection with gap year alums. Monica Andrews has made a unique contribution to the field through her dedication to gap year research and through bringing to life the stories of gap year alums and their parents.

We greatly appreciate the contributions of Bob Dannenhold of Colleology and Sam Bull from LEAPNOW who were willing to share their observations on the impact of gap years, and facilitate access to a greater number of alums. The journey would not be complete without Nick Germanacos, founder of ITHAKA, and his insights into American gappers over the years. Carol Madison provided valuable personal and professional perspective on Americans abroad as did Abigail Falik on global citizenship.

Our thanks go to our partners at SHL, especially Kevin Kerrigan, Paul Levett, and James Bywater in the UK; and Nels Wroe and Hennie Kriek in the U.S.

Eva Brann has been a guiding light in so many ways, especially in helping us see the connection between liberal education and lessons from the real world.

Thank you to Kay Shaw Nelson for her example as a master author. Adam Haigler, our original gapper, and Allison Haigler, a provisional gapper, provided support as reviewers of the survey and analysts. Rachel Haigler has been an advocate for the gap year alternative, particularly in the context of her dedication to service. We thank her for lending her design talent to this project.

ABOUT THE AUTHORS

Karl Haigler and Rae Nelson have a combined fifty years of experience in the fields of education policy and practice.

Karl has served as Director of the Adult Literacy Initiative for the U.S. Department of Education and as Special Advisor for the Governor of Mississippi on literacy and workforce development issues. He has been a teacher, high school principal, and college counselor.

Rae served as Associate Director of Education Policy at The White House and Executive Director of the Center for Workforce Education, a not-for-profit affiliate of the U.S. Chamber of Commerce.

They are co-authors of *The Gap-Year Advantage: Helping Your Child Benefit from Time Off Before or During College* (St. Martin's Griffin).

If you are interested in more information about the research, survey, or anything else in the book – or would like to talk about gap years – please contact us!

Website: www.haiglerenterprises.com

Contact Information:

Karl@haiglerenterprises.com
Rae@haiglerenterprises.com

INDEX

A Brief History of Time, 160
Action Without Borders, 141
AFS, 99, 118
African Global Academy, 187
Alliance for Excellent Education, 58
American Gap Association, 17, 29, 56, 108, 118, 236
AmeriCorps, 17, 94, 97, 110, 141, 150, 152, 153 – 154, 155, 156, 161, 163, 164, 166, 169, 238
Andrews, Monica, 19, 257
Anti-Americanism, 193 – 194
Appalachian State University, 102
Appalachian Trail, 28, 202
Arnett, Jeffrey J., 65, 110
Australia, 14, 28, 45, 103, 107, 113, 153, 159, 160, 183, 188, 190, 203, 238
Bard College, 220
Barnard College, 45, 70
Belize, 14
Bien Cuit, 132
Blinknow.org, 212
Bloch, Deborah, 52
Bloch, Julia, iii, 43 – 44, 51 – 52, 227, 230
Bolivia, 109
Boston University, 68
Botstein, Leon, 220, 223
Boulder Outdoor Survival School, 109
Brann, Eva, 65 – 66

Brazil, 226
Bridge Year, 17, 18
Broh, Lea, 100 – 101
Broh, Tony, 100
Brown, Michael, 94, 98, 242
Brown University, 16, 80, 183
Brownstein, Michael, 98
Buddhism, 43
Bull, Neil, 8, 14 – 15, 63
Bull, Holly, 15
Bull, Mimi, 15
Bureau of Labor Statistics, 1
Bush, George H. W., 152
Byrne, Matt, 112, 139 – 140
Camp, Courtney, 167 – 168
Canada, 76, 115, 153, 182, 226
Cannon, Clare, 59 – 60
Cannon, Wes, 59 – 60, 65, 113, 215
Carolina Alumni Review, 135
Carolina United, 162
Carpe Diem Education, 17, 49, 115
Center for Interim Programs, LLC, 8, 15, 19, 29, 36, 56, 63, 241 – 242
Central College, 95
Charles Schwab, 104
Chile, 14, 28, 101, 102, 173, 180, 181
City Year, Inc., 2, 7, 19, 33 – 34, 48, 77, 94 – 95, 97, 100, 116, 136, 141,
    155, 161 – 163, 164, 165, 208, 212, 213, 217, 228, 229, 242 – 243
Claremont Graduate University, 146, 222
Clark University, 65, 70, 98, 110
Clemson University, 8, 60, 61
Clinton, Bill, 17, 152
College credit, 98 – 99
Collegeology, 19, 243
College of Charleston, The, 68 – 69, 70
College Board, 90, 91
Colleges (attended after gap year), 70 – 71
Colorado College, 69 – 70

Conference Board, 144, 156

Conservation Volunteers Australia, 159

Consultants and counselors, 27, 56, 236

Coping with Anti-Americanism: A Guide to Getting the Most Out of Studying Abroad, 193

Corporation for National and Community Service, 153 – 154, 165

Costa Rica, 2, 64, 70, 101, 103, 106, 107, 183, 187, 194, 195, 196, 199, 203, 221

Credit Card Accountability, Responsibility, and Disclosure Act (CARD), 106

Credit cards, 104 – 105

Creech, William, Sr., 167

Crete, 40

Csikszentmihalyi, Mihaly, 145 – 146, 222

CVS, 228

Cyzgy, 162

Czerwinski, Thomas, 212 – 213

Dalai Lama, 43, 51

Dartmouth College, 64

Davidson College, 32, 70, 80

Deferrals, 68 – 69

Delahunt, Pierce, 226 – 227

Demuth, Bathsheba, 76 – 77, 80, 217

Doyne, Kate, 47 – 48, 211 – 212

Doyne, Maggie, 212

Ducey, Charles, 15

Duke University, 63, 64, 95

Dynamy, 19, 98, 131 – 133, 215, 238, 244

Dyson, Eris, 116, 228 – 229

Echo Hill Outdoor School, 96

Egypt, 102, 112, 180, 181

Eisner, David, 154

Emerging Adulthood, 65, 110

Emerson College, 7, 70, 139

Emory University, 70, 213

Evans, Katherine, 134 – 135

Evergreen State College, 69, 70, 95, 114

Ewing, Ben, 170, 178 – 179
Falik, Abigail, 170 – 171
Fiji, 73, 103, 107, 183, 184, 188
Financial awareness, 104 – 106
Finding Flow: The Psychology of Engagement with Everyday Life, 222
Fitzsimmons, William, 15
Fox, Colin, 6. 9
France, 97, 153, 219
Free Application for Federal Student Aid (FAFSA), 87
Free, Elissa, 36 – 37
Free, Ann Cottrell, 36
FreshMinds Talent, 159
Frontiers of Justice, 176
Fundraising, 99
Gap Activity Projects, 13
GAPPL, 18
Gap year
    Choosing gap year options, 26 – 27, 117
    Colleges attended after gap year, 70 – 71
    Definition, 9, 233 – 234, 240
    Growing trend, 12
    Logistics, 29 – 30
    Origins, 13 – 15
    Research overview, 18
    Reasons to take, 10 – 11
GapYear.com, 13
Gap-Year Advantage: Helping Your Child Benefit from Time Off Before or During College, 3, 4
Gelman, Rita Golden, 87
Genzlinger, Owen, 82 – 83, 104, 217
Germanacos, Nick, 40 – 41, 42
George Foundation, 200
Germany, 181
Ghana, 46
Gilbert, Allison, 216
Global Citizen Year, 97, 170
Global Crossroads, 98

Global Gap Year Fellowships, 18, 98
Global Learning Across Borders, 72, 178, 219
Global Routes, 99, 194
Goucher College, 138
Graham, Carol Madison, 193
Great Eight Competencies, 125 – 129, 129, 136, 214 – 217, 237
Greece, 8, 37, 40, 42, 101, 191, 221
Grinnell College, 36, 70
Griffiths, Tom, 13
Guatemala, 54, 183
Habitat for Humanity, 47, 211
Haidt, Jonathan, 48, 226
Haigler, Adam, 1, 2, 3, 4, 69, 95, 99, 114 – 115, 163, 194 – 197, 220 – 221
Haigler, Allison, 115
Hamilton College, 45, 70
Hampshire College, 47, 70
Happiness Hypothesis, The, 48, 226
Harris, Cristina, 34 – 35, 52, 219 – 220
Harvard College, 15, 66, 247
Harvard Law School, 94, 242
Harvard University, 70, 151
Harvard Crimson, 187
Hawking, Stephen, 160
Heifer Project, 133
HelpArgentina, 80, 81, 143
Hendren, Catherine, 32, 34, 161 – 163
Hendren, Matt, 2, 32 – 34, 161 – 163
Higher Education Debt Project, 105
Hildebrand, Cindy, 190
Hildebrand, Lucas, 190
Hobsons/Trendence, 121, 123, 124 – 127, 129, 146, 214
Holland, 153
Hollister, Chip, 199
Hollister, Lily, 199
Home for the Destitute and Dying, 198
Honduras, 183
Horn, Stephanie, 192 – 193

Howard, Merrell & Partners, 19, 246

Huffington Post, 97

Hughes, Ceci, 95, 96

Hugo, Beverly, 202

Hureau, Maggie, 77 –78, 164 – 165, 217

Impink, Emma, 23 – 24, 54, 176 – 177, 210

India, 33, 36 – 37, 43 – 44, 45, 51, 72, 81, 107, 108, 177 – 178, 198, 100, 201, 202, 215, 222

Institute for Cultural Ecology, 107, 183, 188

Institute for College Access and Success, 92

Institute for Educational Studies, 185

Institute of International Education, 185

International Institute for Education Studies, 185

International Year of the Volunteer, 153

Internship Year College Credit Option (Dynamy), 98

Involvement Volunteers, 107

Ireland, 102, 180, 181, 238

IslandWood, 115

Israel, 202, 204

Italy, 35, 143, 163, 183, 219, 221

ITHAKA, 8, 40 – 41, 42

Ivy, Amy, 174, 224

Ivy, Caroline, 173 – 174, 175 – 176, 216

James, Leigh, 112, 225

James, William, 151

Japan, 153

Jefferson's Children: Education and the Promise of American Culture, 220

Johnson, Mark, 38

Jones, Andrew, 121 – 122, 124, 129

Kaelin, Fred, 131

Kane, Hannah, 136, 141

Kelly, Megan, 6, 7, 9, 75, 77, 109

Kennedy, John, 152

Khazei, Alex, 94, 242

Kickstarter, 99

Kimmel, Will, 23, 49 – 51, 53 – 54

Kiwanis, 152
Knight, Ethan, 17
Krass, Daniel, 63 – 64, 224
Krass, Debbie, 64, 137
Krass, Rebecca (Becca), 63 – 64, 65, 224
Lady Washington, 31, 32, 96, 97
Lakoff, George, 38
Lansing, Gerrit, 41, 42 – 43
Lasarek, Joanna, 36
Latino, Roberto, 53, 142, 144
Lattitude Global Volunteering, 13
Lauch, Andrew, 200 – 202
Lauch, Dennis, 200 – 202
Lawrence University, 202, 203, 204
LEAPNOW, 19, 47, 107, 183, 211, 245
Let's Get Global, 87
Levine, Jackie, 208 – 209, 210
Lewis, Mary McGrath, 15
Lions Clubs, 152
Live New Zealand, 188
Lobel, Louis, 207, 222
Lofgren, David, 31 – 32, 52 – 53, 95, 96 – 97, 217, 219
Magic Carpet Rides, 208
Maine Rose, 202
Manning, Robert D., 105
Massachusetts Institute of Technology (MIT), 16
Masters, Charmaine, 197, 198
Masters, Cory, 197 – 198
Metaphors We Live By, 38
Mexico, 14, 40, 80, 112, 226
Middlebury College, 16, 70, 78, 135
Milkround Graduate Recruitment Survey, 121, 122 – 123, 129
Miller, Carly, 45 – 46, 48
Miller, Eric, 159 – 161
Monteverde Institute, 203
Montiglio, Silvia, 191
Moore, Stuart, 60 – 61, 65

Moore, Tom, 60, 61 – 62
Morehead-Cain Scholar Program, 98
Mother Teresa, 33
Moynihan, Alison, 89, 109, 113
National and Community Service Act of 1990, 152
National and Community Service Trust Act, 17, 152
National Council of State Legislatures, 57, 58, 92
National Outdoor Leadership School, 82, 98, 185
National Republican Congressional Committee, 43
Naugle, Markus, 208
Nepal, 43, 44, 51, 107, 212
New York Film Academy, 82
New York Times, The, 14, 17, 78
New Zealand, 2, 7, 14, 72, 75, 81, 82, 83, 100, 103, 107, 109, 112, 114, 139, 140, 188, 203, 204, 205, 215, 221
Nooter, Amanda, 35 – 38 , 39, 191 – 192
Northeastern University, 70, 95
Notre Dame College, 163, 228
Nussbaum, Martha, 176
Obama, Barrack, 106
Obrero, Teresa, 6, 7 – 8, 163
Ohio Valley University, 95
Olson, Kathy, 143, 163
O'Neil, Erin, 73 – 74, 113, 119, 134, 182 – 184, 221
Outward Bound, 60, 215
Owen, Seth, 135 – 136
Oxford Tutorial College, 7, 28, 39 – 40, 43, 75, 80, 192, 193
Pacific Village Institute, 43
Pakistan, 198
Paying for a Gap Year Blog, 118
Peace Corps, 110, 152, 200, 201, 202
Peace Villages Foundation, 100
Pedrick, Peter, 13
Peru, 47, 178, 194, 195, 197, 223
Pine Mountain Kentucky Settlement School, 167
Pioneer Project, 115, 245 – 246
Pitzer College, 70, 201

PlanetGapYear, 29, 56
Pedrick, Peter, 13
Prescott College, 70, 95
President's Higher Education Community Service Honor Roll, 166
Prince Harry, 14
Prince William, 14
Princeton University, 16, 17, 18, 63, 71, 95, 179, 180, 267
Project on Student Debt, 92
Pulitzer, Sarah, 106 – 108
Ramdial, Sareeta, 202 – 204
Redwoods National Park, 190
Refai, Malaka, 102, 112, 179 – 181, 222
Reverse culture shock, 48
Review of Gap Year Provision, 121 – 122
Rice University, 167, 171
Robert Half International, 158
Rochester Institute of Technology, 105
Rogers, Chelsea, 221
Rotary, 152
Rosseau, Andrew, 218 – 219
Rousseau, Noel, 218 – 219
Rugby Football Union, 14
St. John's College, 8, 65, 71, 185, 189,
St. John's University, 185
Sallie Mae, 90, 91
San Francisco State University, 35, 71, 80
Sarah Lawrence College, 71, 107, 108
Schneider, Barbara, 145
Scholarships, 97 – 98, 117
School of the World, 187
SCUBA, 82
Shenandoah National Park, 135
Sheridan School, 135
SHL Group Ltd., 19, 124, 125, 127, 214, 237, 241, 249
Shoaf, Amanda, 101 – 102
Shoaf, Kathy, 101 – 102
Silva Project, 91

Silverberg, Mary, 109
Silverberg, Shoshanna (Shanna), 46 – 47, 108 – 109, 239
Siwicky, Julie, 72 – 73, 177 – 178, 215,
Skidmore College, 71, 78
Smith, Charlotte, 41 – 42
South Africa, 23, 24, 28, 47, 50, 53, 54, 176, 187, 210, 249
Southeastern University, 95
Spain, 203
Spartan College of Aeronautics and Technology, 71, 83
State of College Savings Survey, 91
Stevens, Parker, 102 – 104, 187 – 189
Student Conservation Association, 95
Student Extended Experiences Consulting, Inc., 19, 246 – 247
Student Intelligence Report, 121, 124 – 125, 127
Student Times, 122
Study abroad programs, 185 – 187
Survey of Parents of College-Bound Freshmen, 90
Swarthmore College, 16
Switzerland, 81
Syracuse University, 95
Tales of a Female Nomad: Living at Large In the World, 87
Tanzania, 103, 187
Teacher of English to Speakers of Other Languages (TESOL), 200
Teel, Jon, 39 – 40, 57, 80 – 81, 143 – 144, 216
Tibet, 43, 44, 107, 187,
Time Out or Burn Out for the Next Generation, 15 – 16, 66
Tocqueville, Alexis de, 151
Tom Brown's Tracker School, 226
Totnes School for Guitar Making, 160
Travelers Worldwide, 187
Tufts University, 16, 71
Tulane University, 71, 74
Turkey, 142
Union College, 71, 95
United Kingdom/Britain, 7, 13 – 14, 20, 39, 70, 71, 75, 99, 107, 120,
    121 – 129, 151, 153

United Nations, 77, 153

United Way, 143, 163

University of Arkansas, 95

University of California, 63, 71, 188, 201, 247

University of Chicago, 145, 176

University of Dar es Salaam, 103, 188

University of Delaware, 95

University of Iowa, 71, 143

University of Minnesota, 8

University of New Hampshire, 71, 175

University of New Mexico, 159

University of North Carolina at Chapel Hill, 16, 18, 32, 71, 98, 117, 134, 162

University of Texas, 82, 213

University of Virginia, 48, 71, 226

University of Washington in St. Louis, 166

University of Wisconsin, 71, 191

Up with People, 102

USA Gap Year Fairs, 12, 17, 56,

U.S. Department of Defense, 237

U.S. Department of Education, 58, 237

U.S. Department of Labor, 237

U.S. Department of State, 206, 237

U.S. Public Interest Research Group, 105

US UK Fulbright Commission, 193

Verde Valley School, 14

Versant Solutions, 158

VisitOz, 45

Wake Forest University, 69

Wall Street Journal, The, 17

Wandering in Ancient Greek Culture, 191

Washington Conservation Corps, 95, 97, 217

Welsh Guards, 14

Wessling, Andrea Chace, 132, 215

Wheatcroft, Kate, 89

Wheelock, Laura, 132 – 133

Where There Be Dragons, 36

Wildlands Studies Program, 40, 80, 188

Williams College, 64, 71, 137

Williams, Harris, 225

Williams, Libba, 225

Women and Thru-Hiking on the Appalachian Trail: Practical Advice from Hundreds of Women Long Distance Hikers, 202

Worcester Rape Crisis, 132

Worldwide Opportunities On Organic Farms (WWOOF), 190, 203

Yahoo! HotJobs, 158

Year Up, 238